LEWIS HAMILTON

LEWIS HAMILTON:
NEW KID ON THE GRID

IAN STAFFORD

MAINSTREAM PUBLISHING

EDINBURGH AND LONDON

First published in Great Briain in 2007 by
MAINSTREAM PUBLISHING COMPANY (EDINBURGH) LTD
7 Albany Street
Edinburgh EH1 3UG

ISBN 9781845963385

A catalogue record for this book is available from the British Library

Text design by Gill McColl

Typeset in Baskerville, Champion and Gill Sans

Printed in Great Britain by
Butler & Tanner, Frome, Somerset

Contents

vodafone
BRIDGESTONE
Mercedes-Benz
Mobil 1
BOSS
HUGO BOSS
JOHNNIE WALKER
aigo
Santander
SAP
MUTUA MADRILEÑA
vodafone

Introduction

Before the Australian Grand Prix in 2007, the traditional curtain-raiser for the Formula One season, it was probably fair to say that few people outside those who worked in motor sport or followed it keenly had even heard of Lewis Carl Hamilton. Sure, he'd appeared on *Blue Peter* as a six-year-old kid playing with remote-controlled cars, and again a few years later as a promising junior kart champion, but even as he rose to prominence in the lower levels of single-seater motor racing, culminating in his winning of the 2006 GP2 world title, people in the street would have had no idea who he was.

Formula One, at least in the eyes of the British general public, was struggling. True, you were always going to get your ardent fans packing the stands at Monaco and Monza, Indianapolis and Interlagos, and even in Barcelona, where Spanish fans could rejoice in double world champion Fernando Alonso. But in Britain, Formula One had lost much of its interest.

It did not help that a British driver had not really threatened to become world champion for 11 years. Formula One was a huge British industry, which other nations joined over the years. Many of the top teams either had been in the past or were currently based in the United Kingdom – McLaren, Williams, Lotus, Brabham. Many of the sport's most iconic names also happened to be British – Sir Stirling Moss, Mike Hawthorn, John Surtees, Graham Hill, Jim Clark, Sir Jackie Stewart, James Hunt, Nigel Mansell, Damon Hill – and all but Moss, famously, had world titles to their names. Even the sport's leading figures – from Formula One Management's Bernie Ecclestone to the FIA president Max Mosley – were British.

There had been other British Grand Prix drivers since Damon Hill had won his world title in 1996, most notably David Coulthard and Jenson Button. Coulthard, still going in 2007, had achieved many feats in his astounding career – two British Grand Prix wins, two wins at Monaco, thirteen race victories in total and more points secured than any other British Formula One driver – but the world title had eluded him over and over again. Button had proved to be a real crowd favourite with consummate skill, but he rarely had a car that was competitive. His third place in the drivers' championship in 2005 for Honda was the best he had achieved, but he still hoped that one day he would drive for a team with a car that would give him the chance to become world champion.

Even still, it had been a long wait for a new champion, and the longer the relative lack of British success had gone on, the more interest in this country had waned. However, things were not quite at crisis point. Although the British Grand Prix at Silverstone was constantly being threatened with the axe due to the circuit's dilapidated condition, it still enjoyed healthy crowds, and ITV's audience figures remained high. Yet there was no doubt that Formula One in the United Kingdom needed an injection from somewhere or someone.

Part of it was Michael Schumacher's fault, although the now retired seven-time world champion was not prepared to hold his hand up simply because he had had the temerity to keep on winning. There had been times when Formula One races had turned into one long procession, and the rules had seemed simple: 20 or 22 cars would start a race that would last around 90 minutes and end after 190 or so miles with Schumacher winning.

Alonso helped turn things around by winning both the 2005 and 2006 world titles with Renault, and with Schumacher announcing his retirement at the end of the 2006 season, the sport, despite recognising the German to be one of the greatest drivers of all time – if not the greatest – was not sorry to see the back of him. Maybe now Formula One could become competitive again, and with Alonso moving to McLaren-Mercedes and the super-quick Kimi Räikkönen replacing Schumacher at Ferrari, almost everyone who had an opinion in the paddock saw it as a straight fight between the Spaniard and the Finn, with Brazil's Felipe Massa, Ferrari's other driver, perhaps making it a three-way battle.

One man – although he was almost still a boy – who nobody considered was the rookie who had just been appointed as McLaren-Mercedes' other Formula One driver. Those in the sport knew that he was good, but the general view was that Hamilton would spend a couple of years learning from the masterful Fernando Alonso. During this time, he would pick up points – and probably a good many of them, too – but his main role would be to support his teammate as he attempted to add to his two world titles, grab some podium finishes, maybe even secure an unlikely victory or two if other cars fell by the wayside and then launch a serious bid for the world title after two or three years in Formula One.

Nothing before the start of the season, not even Hamilton's impressive times in testing, changed this view. Indeed, when he was unveiled at the all-singing, all-dancing McLaren launch in Valencia in January 2007, the difference between him and Alonso was remarkable. In front of his home support, the Spaniard appeared to be exactly what he was: the double world champion. Indeed, he was the only driver on the 2007 grid with a world title to his name, and his manner towards Hamilton was bordering on paternal. This was not in any way patronising. At the time, Alonso would have been delighted to have a young, eager and clearly talented teammate who would undoubtedly do his bit to help secure him another world title. But it was equally obvious that the Spaniard did not see Hamilton's impact on the sport coming, which goes a long way to explaining the difficulty he had when he realised too late that among his greatest rivals would be not just Räikkönen, but his own junior colleague at McLaren as well.

Back in January 2007, Hamilton came across as a beaming kid in a candy store. He had created his own luck by having the confidence as a young boy to tell McLaren boss Ron Dennis that one day he would be driving for him, and here he was, many years later, resplendent in a Vodafone McLaren-Mercedes race suit, standing beside the double world champion in front of the new MP4-22 car, revealed during the grand ceremony in Valencia. Hamilton blinked repeatedly as the flashbulbs lit up the night sky. After all those years of dreaming, and all those years of racing, he had arrived. To the outside world, Hamilton had become a Formula One driver overnight. For Hamilton, this journey had taken 14 years, from the first day he raced a kart and revealed astounding hand-eye coordination and a determination to win.

If a screenwriter had nervously sat down in a Hollywood producer's office and suggested what then followed as a movie project, it would have been the kind of script a film mogul would have laughed at before ripping to shreds. The first black driver in Formula One went on to break myriad records and took the championship down to the last race to decide whether he would become the first rookie in the sport's history to be crowned world champion. If that was not enough, there were tensions and controversy like never before, and this is in a sport in which tension and controversy are integral. All of the talking points seemed to surround Hamilton, his relationship with his world-champion teammate, who struggled to deal with the fact that a rookie appeared to have the beating of him, or his team. From spy scandals that would dominate the middle part of the season to a complete breakdown in the relationship between the two drivers, and from attempts on various occasions to have Hamilton thrown out of races – or at least have points docked or grid positions dented – to incidents galore on the track at high speed, the 2007 season was an unforgettable maelstrom of fast cars, personality clashes and so many twists and turns both on and off the circuit that it was probably just as well the season came to an end in Brazil.

FACING PAGE: A brave new dawn – rookie Lewis Hamilton and double world champion Fernando Alonso pose at the launch of the McLaren MP4-22 in Valencia. Neither could have foretold the amazing season about to unfold.

Has there ever been a season like it? The answer is a definite no. And has any rookie ever made the impact Lewis Hamilton did in 2007? Again, the response is in the negative. From a podium finish in his first-ever Formula One Grand Prix to four consecutive second places and two successive wins in just his sixth and seventh Grands Prix, followed by more podiums, two more victories and finally high drama in the last two races of the season, and from a scandal so big that McLaren ended up being expelled from the constructors' championship to a row so personal that it is inconceivable that Alonso and Hamilton will ever be real friends again, Lewis Hamilton has seen and learned more in one year than he is likely to for the rest of what promises to

be a wonderfully successful career in Formula One.

Perhaps the most pertinent point is that 2007 was year one of Hamilton's Formula One experience. To think that he achieved what he did in such circumstances must be frightening for the other drivers on the Formula One grid. He can only get better and better. At 22 years of age, he is by no means the finished article. Just how good he can become is a mouth-watering prospect for British motor-racing fans – indeed, British sports fans everywhere – and for Formula One, the resurrection of which in 2007 can be largely attributed to the emergence of a new superstar. This, then, is the story of how Lewis Hamilton took the world of Formula One by storm in 2007.

From Boy

to Formula One Driver

He was not to know it at the time, of course, but when Davidson Hamilton made the momentous decision to leave his native Grenada and emigrate to 1950s Britain, the seeds for the amazing 2007 Formula One season were first sown. His son Anthony grew up in troubled times, especially as a young black man trying to earn his way in a society that was not entirely welcoming. While friends and contemporaries turned to a life of crime, Anthony rolled up his sleeves, revealing a work ethic that would, many years later, rear its head again in the form of an exciting motor-racing driver who would turn Formula One on its head.

Anthony Hamilton took a job as a British Rail clerk and then sought to better himself by studying at night school before establishing his own IT consultancy in London, which he recently tried to sell. But by then he had a son who looked destined to become a star.

Lewis Carl Hamilton was born in the Hertfordshire town of Tewin in January 1985 to Anthony and his first wife Carmen. He was named after Carl Lewis, the legendary American athlete who won gold at the 1984, 1988, 1992 and 1996 Olympic Games, as well as numerous medals at the World Athletics Championships. When Lewis was aged just two, his parents separated. He lived with his mother until he was ten years old, before moving in with his father and his second wife Linda. As a result, Lewis gained a half-brother called Nicholas, who became his greatest friend and companion, despite being six years younger.

At five years old, Lewis Hamilton was bullied at school. 'It was horrible, but I told my dad I wanted to start karate so I could protect myself,' Hamilton recalled. 'The bullying stopped, and, more importantly, I got real self-confidence.' By 12, he had become a black belt.

His love affair with motor racing also began at the age of five when he first played with remote-controlled cars on the balcony of his father's flat in Stevenage, where he slept over at weekends. By six, he was beating adults, became a national champion and made his first television appearance on BBC's *Blue Peter*, racing the cars around the famous garden. 'It was a big day out,' Hamilton said. 'I think I was at least 20 years younger than the other contestants, but I won.'

That same year, the first glimpse of his natural talent behind a wheel became evident when on holiday in Spain. Taking the wheel of an electric car, he showed a natural ease driving, which did not go unnoticed by Anthony. Fascinated to see whether his son's hand-eye coordination could be transferred into racing, he took him along to Rye House kart track in Hoddesdon, just south of Stevenage. In his first trial run in a kart, Lewis Hamilton, aged six, lapped his father. Later that session, he had a shunt, emerging with a bloodied nose. Anthony assumed that would be that and his son would never sit in a kart again, but little Lewis jumped straight back into the kart and resumed.

His father had seen enough. Anthony bought Lewis a second-hand kart complete with race suit and helmet for Christmas, just before his son's eighth birthday. The plan, in part, was to help motivate him to work hard at school, but it soon became apparent which direction his son would be taking. There were no plans by the family to kick-start a career in motor sport, but Lewis had already made up his mind. 'As soon as I started to race karts, I knew I wanted to be a Formula One driver,' he admits.

At each stage in Hamilton's fledgling career as a junior racing driver, his father had to change his stance. Having bought Lewis a second-hand kart, they just pitched up at circuits to race, and Anthony watched his son, with no experience, win his first six novice cadet kart races. When he lost his novice tag and competed in his first full-plate race, Lewis won that as well. It was slowly dawning on Anthony that his son possessed two special skills: the ability to drive a kart better than the rest and a deep hunger to win. 'Lewis has wanted to win for as long as I can remember,' says Anthony. 'If he doesn't win, it really grates on him.'

From the age of six onwards, both father and son watched as many Formula One Grands Prix on television as possible, and it was because of this that Ayrton Senna, the dashing Brazilian world champion, became the boy's hero.

What was at first a weekend hobby fast became a serious pursuit, and by the end of 1993 Lewis had become a well-known figure in junior karting,

impressing enough to be signed up by Martin Hines, who owned the kart-manufacturing company Zipkart, based close to the Rye House circuit. Hines, well-known for his good eye for talent, signed up Hamilton and Gary Paffett, who later became McLaren-Mercedes' test driver for the 2007 Formula One season. Hines supplied Lewis with his kart chassis throughout his time in karting, and when other equipment suppliers and sponsors heard of this precocious kid they soon came knocking on Anthony Hamilton's door. As a result, the Hamiltons, who were hardly wealthy, were aided financially in Lewis's formative racing years.

It was when Lewis was ten that his now famous meeting with Ron Dennis took place. Neither of them knew it at the time, but it would prove to be a life-changing moment for them both. Lewis had been invited to the British AutoSport awards in London, because he had just won the British Kart Championship at cadet level. Dennis was there as the guest of honour. The Hamiltons could not afford the formal suit required for the function, so Lewis borrowed a silky green suit from a karting friend. Despite this, he showed how unfazed he was by circulating around the tables with his autograph book collecting signatures. Having snared Damon Hill, John Surtees, Colin McRae and Richard Burns, he walked straight up to Dennis, introduced himself, asked for his autograph and made the bemused chairman and CEO of the McLaren Group a promise. 'I told Ron my name, asked for his signature, as well as his address and telephone number, and then told him that one day I wanted to race for him and become world champion.' Dennis scribbled in the boy's book, 'Phone me in nine years' time, and we'll sort something out.' It later transpired that Dennis, suitably impressed by the small boy's ambition, had him checked out. From that point onwards, he kept an eye on Lewis's progress.

Not long after this, the story of Lewis Hamilton's yellow helmet was born. So concerned was Anthony for his son's safety that he wanted to ensure he knew exactly where Lewis was out on the track at any given time. 'Having a yellow helmet meant he would stand out among every other driver,' Anthony explained. His son has worn it ever since.

Over the next few years, as he turned from young boy to teenager, Lewis continued to dominate every

LEFT: A ten-year-old future world champion? Lewis Hamilton waits for the fog to lift before a day's karting in Northamptonshire on 10 December 1995.

ABOVE: GPS champ – Hamilton in action in 2006 in the GP2 race in Barcelona.

race category he entered, from cadet-class champion to winning the McLaren-Mercedes Champions of the Future series, until, after a word from Martin Hines, Hamilton first tested and then became a works driver for the Topkart Comer organisation in Italy.

By then, he had Ron Dennis on board. The McLaren Group chairman telephoned Anthony and offered to help fund Lewis's progress through the lower echelons of motor sport. The boy had just turned 13 and was told the happy news when he returned home from school. Suddenly, a career in motor sport became a real possibility.

The help from Dennis made an immense difference. Lewis admitted in 2007 that 'without that support from Ron in the early days I would never be in Formula One today'. However, his parents still had to find a great deal of money from somewhere, and after taking up all kinds of extra jobs – including erecting 'For Sale' signs for £15 a go – Anthony and Linda decided to take redundancy to further pay Lewis's way.

On the kart circuits of Europe, Hamilton continued to blaze his way to victory. At 15, he won every round of the Formula A European Championship and the World Cup in Japan, and he was crowned karting's youngest-ever number-one driver, a record he holds to this day. He had also been signed up to the McLaren driver development support programme, which included a contract with the option of a future Formula One seat. In 2000, the British Racing Drivers' Club labelled him a 'Rising Star' member, and one year later his car-racing career began in the British Formula Renault Winter Series, in which he finished fifth.

This, in turn, led to a full year's campaign in 2002 in Formula Renault UK. Hamilton finished the season third, with three wins and three poles, but the following year he was champion, with a staggering ten wins. By 2004, he had progressed to the Formula Three Euroseries. Hamilton finished the season in fifth place with one race victory, but he had done enough to convince McLaren to let him test at Silverstone at the end of the year.

It was in 2005 that the world of motor sport knew for sure that they had a future champion on their hands. Moving to reigning Euroseries champions ASM, he dominated the Formula Three championship, winning 15 of the 20 rounds. Not surprisingly, he then made the jump up to GP2 for the 2006 season after being signed up by ART Grand Prix. Not for the first time, and definitely not for the last, Hamilton had joined a winning team. ART were the 2005 champions, and Lewis duly won the 2006 championship in his first season in GP2, with five wins, including two double wins at the Nürburgring and at Silverstone as well as a victory in Monaco.

Hamilton was now within a sniff of Formula One, and a slice of good fortune was soon to fall his way. Both of McLaren's Formula One drivers, Kimi Räikkönen and Juan Pablo Montoya, were leaving the team at the end of the 2006 season. Räikkönen went to Ferrari, where he was going to attempt to fill the sizeable vacancy left by Michael Schumacher. Montoya, disillusioned with his failure to make his mark in Formula One, returned to American motor sport.

There were many weeks of speculation concerning who would join double world champion Fernando Alonso, who had left Renault to join McLaren. Hamilton was in the frame, but so too were test driver Pedro de la Rosa, former kart colleague Gary Paffett and even former double world champion Mika Häkkinen.

Hamilton discovered his fate on 23 September 2006. Dennis had invited the young driver to his house to break the happy news. 'You're going to be our second driver for next year,' he told Hamilton.

The world of motor sport did not know what to think. Everybody had seen what the kid had achieved in the lower levels of the sport. He was clearly a born winner, but asking him to drive for McLaren as a rookie alongside Fernando Alonso appeared to most people to be a gamble. David Coulthard even publicly stated that Hamilton should have been given a year's testing first. But Ron Dennis and the rest of his team at McLaren had seen enough. Besides, they had a hunch Lewis Hamilton might cause a bigger stir than people could ever have imagined. As hunches go, this proved to be bigger and better than even they could have expected.

TEAM HAMILTON

Anthony Hamilton, father

The driving force behind Lewis, a father, mentor and now manager, Anthony Hamilton is the archetypal racing dad. He threw everything at funding his son's motor-racing career, famously holding down three jobs at one time, as well as being his son's kart mechanic. 'I was spending my annual salary on the kart, engines and equipment,' Anthony recalled. 'I relied on credit cards and an overdraft.' You could say it has paid off. He will sit down with McLaren-

Mercedes immediately after the final race of the season in Brazil to renegotiate his son's contract. The £340,000 Hamilton currently earns a year is expected to rise to £10 million, which would equate to an awful lot of 'For Sale' signs. 'I owe everything to my dad,' Hamilton junior admitted. 'We're a team.'

Nicholas Hamilton, half-brother

An unlikely but vital link in the Lewis Hamilton chain is his 16-year-old half-brother Nicholas, who suffers from cerebral palsy. Nicholas, Anthony's son from his second marriage, is described by Lewis as his 'greatest inspiration' and was present at a number of the 2007 Grands Prix. They are the best of friends and hang out with one another as much as they can, often playing on the PlayStation, racing around computerised versions of the real circuits that Lewis encountered in his first year in Formula One, enabling the driver to carry out research. 'I think Nicholas is an amazing lad, and I really love to do things for him,' Lewis explains. 'He loves a challenge, and he's got steeper challenges to face yet, but he fights so hard, and if he can fight every day, then so can I. Nicholas is my greatest inspiration. I look at him, and that puts my life into perspective. We are very close. I race for him. He's what keeps me up there and keeps me motivated.'

Ron Dennis, McLaren Group chairman and CEO

Chairman, CEO and part-owner of the McLaren Group, Ron Dennis, the 60-year-old former mechanic for Jack Brabham, has been Hamilton's other great mentor and supporter, and their first meeting at the British Autosport Awards will go down in the annals of sporting history. Three years later, and after three successive British kart titles, Hamilton received a call from Dennis at home offering him support and sponsorship. 'To a degree, that changed our whole lives, because suddenly Lewis had an opportunity to make a career in motor sport,' admits Anthony Hamilton. Since then, Dennis and McLaren have invested £5 million in helping Hamilton become the driver he is today, and while a disgruntled Fernando Alonso seems likely to leave the Woking-based team, the spectacular Hamilton and Dennis partnership looks set to continue for quite some time yet.

Martin Whitmarsh, McLaren-Mercedes CEO

The 49-year-old Whitmarsh has played a vital role in McLaren's young-driver scheme and helped to draw up the detailed programme that Hamilton followed studiously from September 2006 until the start of the 2007 season to ensure he was ready for Formula One. 'I think what McLaren has basically developed is a very sound understanding of what a driver needs to do in order to improve himself to the sort of level required to perform in Formula One,' he explains. 'Lewis turned himself into the driver he is today. We just provided the support and the situation in which he could hone his skills. From day one, Lewis impressed us with his level of commitment. If he hadn't, we wouldn't have invested a penny in him.'

Phil Prew, McLaren race engineer

The key relationship on race day is between Hamilton and his race engineer Phil Prew, a long-term McLaren employee who worked with Kimi Räikkönen during the 2006 season. Prew is the voice on the radio link from the pits, advising on how a race is unfolding, but he was also involved in the months before the season's start, preparing his new driver. 'Ron and Martin gave me the job, when it was confirmed last November that Lewis would be driving for us, of turning him from a GP2 driver into a Formula One driver,' Prew admits. 'Actually, the brief was more specific than that. I was told to have him ready to score a podium in Melbourne.' Prew provided Hamilton with detailed dossiers on racing Formula One cars and each circuit, and now Hamilton receives another dossier after each race, reviewing how he and the car performed. 'Lewis is still developing his style,' adds Prew. 'But he's an expert when it comes to racing skills.'

Dr Kerry Spackman, neuroscientist

This 50-year-old motorcyclist and waterskier from New Zealand is a former mathematician who turned neuroscientist after a chance meeting with Sir Jackie Stewart 15 years ago that sparked an interest in the skills of racing drivers. He has worked with Hamilton for four years and helps operate the 'secret' simulator that prepared Lewis for Formula One. 'Today's Formula One car does things instantaneously, and the brain can't keep up,' Spackman explains. 'The idea is thus to rewire its circuits, to supercharge its processes, so that it's more suited to the task. The task is to turn it, if you like, from a computer into a supercomputer. Lewis obviously has talent, but he's a vastly superior driver now because he's learned how to learn. It means he

doesn't just repeat the same old habits. Every experience is analysed, understood and filed away. I'd say Lewis has a pretty well-rounded emotional system.'

Adam Costanzo, personal trainer/physiotherapist

An Australian from Brisbane, Costanzo is the member of McLaren's human-performance laboratory who was assigned to Hamilton to ensure his fitness was at its optimum for the start of the Formula One season. Known to be a man who pushes his clients hard, Costanzo has transformed his pupil into one of the fittest drivers on the grid, if not the fittest. 'Lewis was already fit, but there was no real structure to his training programme,' Costanzo explained, having built up a good rapport with Hamilton in 2006 before joining him on the race circuit in 2007. 'That's one of the biggest areas where we've helped him.' Just as every part of the car is monitored, so too are the drivers' individual performances and a detailed record of their fitness is kept. 'We worked hard together every day over the winter, focusing first on strengthening his neck and lower back, then on his all-round cardiovascular fitness by running, swimming and cycling.'

Norbert Haug, president of Mercedes-Benz motor sport

Haug worked with Hamilton in Formula Three Euro-series and spotted his outstanding quality early on. The German has guided Hamilton's career ever since, acting as another mentor.

Paddy Lowe, McLaren engineering director

Lowe is responsible for ensuring that all parts of the car operate as one and that it is reliable. He is the man who accepts that the buck stops with him.

Dave Ryan, McLaren team manager

Ryan works more on the administrative side of things at McLaren but was a constant companion to Hamilton during 2007 due to his incessant trips to see the stewards.

Paul James, McLaren head mechanic

A Welshman (originally) known as 'Taffy', James is in charge of car set-up. His other role is to catch the champagne bottle Hamilton receives for finishing in a podium place. This amounted to quite a few bottles over the course of the 2007 season, and James is proud of the fact that he didn't drop a single bottle.

Race 1

Australian Grand Prix

Melbourne

Sunday, 18 March 2007

Attendance: 105,000
Weather: sunny, 22 °C
Track temperature: 40 °C
Number of laps: 58
Circuit length: 3.295 miles
Race distance: 191.11 miles
Fastest lap: Kimi Räikkönen, 1:25.235 (lap 41)

Hamilton 3rd, 6 points (6)

MELBOURNE GRAND PRIX CIRCUIT

Lewis Hamilton's official entrance into the world of Formula One took place via a water taxi on Thursday, 15 March, when he arrived at a beachfront restaurant in the Melbourne suburb of St Kilda to be met by a horde of waiting cameramen and photographers.

It could have been straight out of a James Bond movie. The sky was blue, the sun shone and the babes, ever-present during the long weekend of a Formula One Grand Prix, greeted Vodafone McLaren-Mercedes' latest driver combo. Fernando Alonso was the double world champion and McLaren's star signing from Renault. Hamilton was the 22-year-old rookie, the second-youngest man to be starting on the grid in Melbourne and the first black driver in the 57 years of the Formula One world championship. Yet the kid seemed as confident and at ease as the legend alongside him.

The next day he would be seen in McLaren's pewter and vermillion MP4-22 car for the first time in free practice. The sport had waited impatiently all winter for the new season to start, and during this time the talking had as usual dominated. Would Kimi Räikkönen step into the retired shoes of Michael Schumacher and fulfil his undoubted potential at Ferrari? Would Felipe Massa, Schumacher's number two, take over his former colleague's mantle? Were BMW Sauber serious players this year? And would Alonso make it a hat-trick of successive world titles? 'I want to win more world titles,' was the Spaniard's ominous message from down under.

Yet no driver was being talked up more than Hamilton. Not necessarily for the upcoming race, but most definitely for the future. The list of former and present greats singing his praises read like a who's who of Formula One. 'I have no qualms in predicting Lewis will be world champion in the next three to five years,' said Nigel Mansell, former Formula One and CART champion. 'It could be earlier. It's not hard to imagine him winning his first Grand Prix this year.'

Sir Jackie Stewart, the former three-time world champion, was another instant fan. 'Lewis is the best-prepared new Formula One driver I've ever seen,' he insisted. 'He has an excellent chance of really stamping his mark on the sport. He's very well-rounded and very skilled.'

David Coulthard, who has scored more Grand

ABOVE: Words of wisdom from mentor Sir Jackie Stewart after first practice in Melbourne.

Prix points than any other British driver, and who would be starting his 13th season in the sport driving for Red Bull, ventured even further. 'Lewis will win a Grand Prix in his first year, and there's no question that he is a future world champion,' he predicted. 'I'll even suggest that he'll be standing on the podium in Melbourne.'

Bernie Ecclestone, the sport's supremo, also joined in with plaudits of his own: 'If you ask me whether I expect a British driver to be world champion in the next five years, I'd say yes and that it will be Hamilton. I'm very pleased he's made it, and I hope that soon he will be regarded like Tiger Woods is in golf, as a champion whose skin colour is not even mentioned any more.'

Even the sponsors were making wild predictions. 'Lewis is a groundbreaker,' said David Wheldon, head of global marketing for Vodafone, McLaren's title sponsor. 'If he fulfils his potential, then, sponsorship-wise, he can be as big as David Beckham.'

So, no pressure then on master Hamilton. Although already in the glare of the Formula One season's build-up, the young man from Hertfordshire appeared at ease with the new life he had just embarked on and the huge weight of expectation. The sporting world expected an impact from him over the next few months, but only in a cameo role behind the major players and a predicted duel between Alonso and Räikkönen, with Massa picking up the scraps. Hamilton, however, had other plans.

'I've never been fazed, and I'm not fazed now,' he reported on the Thursday evening. 'I'm in a great position. I respect Fernando, and I realise my position in the team, but at the end of the day I'm here to win, and I'll be working towards this. I have to be realistic, though. If I were to get a podium this year, it would be really amazing, so I've got to work towards that. My aim in Melbourne is to finish, preferably in the points. It would be great to have a steady first race, but it's not going to be easy.'

The lead-up to Melbourne had been encouraging. There had been a 165-mph crash in Valencia earlier in the year, but, apart from that little mishap, Hamilton had been only a hair's breadth away from Alonso in testing. 'Testing has been going well,' he reported. 'I've been really happy with how I've gelled with the team and my engineer Phil Prew. We've done race simulations, including pit stops and other race-weekend activities. Everyone within the team is really keen to push hard now.'

FACING PAGE: Alone with his thoughts – Hamilton dreams of a podium in Melbourne.

Hamilton also revealed that he had spent some of his time preparing for his Grand Prix debut by playing computer games with his disabled brother. He had never raced for real around Melbourne's Albert Park street circuit, but believed his experience of competing in the virtual version against his brother gave him a good grounding. 'My brother Nicholas and I have always been playing Formula One games on the computer, and now I'm going to be one of those cars in those games,' he said. 'At this time of year, I've always looked forward to the first Grand Prix, getting up early and watching it, but now I'm actually going to be on the grid. There are many different emotions, but excitement is definitely the main one. When I get on the grid in Melbourne and am sat in front of the red lights, it will be the best moment so far in my life. Nicholas will be very happy as well. He's seven years younger and a great character. He might have cerebral palsy, but he definitely wants to do something special with his life. He gives me real perspective. He's the one member of my family who'll keep my feet on the ground.'

One day later and the Hamilton family were smiling after Lewis took to first practice like a Formula One veteran. The sunshine of the beach entrance had given way to grey clouds and rain, a test for most drivers on the grid, let alone a rookie. A Spyker veered off the track, followed by a Toro Rosso. Alonso cruised through lap after lap, while Hamilton waited for the track to dry. Just half an hour remained of morning practice when history was finally made: Lewis Hamilton's Grand Prix career was up and running. He had expressed concern about spinning off during his very first practice session. Instead, he went under one minute forty seconds on his fourth lap, a time quicker than Alonso had achieved in twelve laps. The afternoon session went even better as the track dried out, the sun shone and the temperature gauge read 22 °C, 33 °C trackside. By Friday night, the rookie was looking ahead to qualifying the following day content in the knowledge that he had been the third-fastest driver on the circuit after a near faultless display on a slippery surface – faster than Coulthard, faster than Giancarlo Fisichella and even faster than his teammate Alonso.

'He's so confident and relaxed it's scary,' muttered

BELOW: It's Hamilton from Felipe Massa in the second practice session in Melbourne.

Anthony Hamilton, Lewis's father and manager. 'When I saw his name on the timing screen, I thought, "That's it. He's here."'

His son was equally excited. 'It's like preparing for the first race at any level,' he said. 'But it was amazing pulling out of the garage and driving along the pit lane and onto the track. I couldn't imagine I'd be third, but Saturday and Sunday are when it matters.'

Hamilton was right, but Saturday's qualifying produced more of the same. In the morning, during more practice in the rain, Hamilton was again third. After lunch, when qualifying got under way, the sun came out, dried the track and the world's greatest drivers vied for the high places on the starting grid.

Ferrari had a mixed afternoon. Kimi Räikkönen sent a warning shot across the McLaren bows by taking pole, but his teammate Massa would be starting the Australian Grand Prix in 16th place after his gearbox failed him. Alonso nudged ahead of his young colleague to take his place alongside Räikkönen on the front row, while Nick Heidfeld grabbed third place in his purposely light BMW

ABOVE: Ferrari's Kimi Räikkönen leads from BMW Sauber's Nick Heidfeld and Hamilton during the Australian Grand Prix.

Sauber. Then came Hamilton in fourth place, in his first-ever Formula One qualifying session and in a heavier car. Tucked right behind Alonso, the British driver bettered Michael Schumacher, who could only start in seventh place at the Belgium Grand Prix on his qualifying debut back in 1991.

'I'm overwhelmed to be on the second row of the grid in my first Grand Prix,' Hamilton declared afterwards. 'It's more than I could have asked for. This is what I prepared myself for during the past 14 years, and I've loved every minute of it. I'm not disappointed in not getting pole. How could I be? This is the pinnacle of the sport, and it is not a sport you can just come into and go straight to the front. It is a lot to take in, but I think I'm dealing with it OK.'

His first weekend in Formula One would get better still, beginning with the very first corner of the Australian Grand Prix. The grid had been cleared of the hundreds of luminaries, dignitaries, pit girls, media figures and mechanics. Hamilton had placed his ear plugs in, closed his visor, gripped his wheel and focused hard on what would be his debut Grand Prix.

Only Giancarlo Baghetti had ever won a Formula One Grand Prix on debut, and that was at Reims in the French Grand Prix back in 1961. By starting in fourth place on the grid, Hamilton stood a chance to emulate this feat. In reality, a decent points finish would be the perfect way to kick-start a career in Formula One. But the start, and the notoriously tight first corner, would be crucial.

In a sense, the Hamilton–Alonso rivalry that grew as the season progressed was born at that very first corner. Räikkönen got away to a clean start out in front to lead, but Heidfeld, behind the Finn, followed in his slipstream to shoot into second place. Alonso was forced to brake behind the German BMW Sauber driver, which gave Hamilton his chance. Using nothing more than sheer instinct hewn out of 14 years of racing and winning, Hamilton moved deftly to his left and to the outside of BMW Sauber's second driver, the talented Pole Robert Kubica, who had started from fifth on the grid. The two McLaren drivers rounded the first corner level, but, in doing so, Hamilton had the better line into the ensuing left-hander and completed the outside pass like a seasoned veteran. This was not driving. This was racing, and it was a move which would be talked about afterwards by many impressed observers within the sport.

Heidfeld, driving light, hence his high qualification, was the first of the leaders to make a scheduled pit stop on lap 14. Räikkönen followed suit five laps later. This proved to be a significant moment in the career of Lewis Hamilton. For the first time, he found himself leading a Formula One Grand Prix, just 19 laps into his career. It would not last long. Räikkönen, in what appeared to be a superior Ferrari, swept back into the lead, which he held until his second pit stop on lap 42. By then, Kubica, running in fourth place, had retired with gearbox problems, Jenson Button, who had been disappointed to start the first Grand Prix of the new season in 14th place on the grid, copped a drive-through penalty for speeding in the pit lane and Felipe Massa was enjoying himself as he carved his way past the less competitive cars from the back of the grid.

On lap forty-three, Hamilton made his second pit stop, which proved to be less successful than Alonso's second pit stop two laps later. Although the Spaniard lost time behind Massa just prior to his stop, Hamilton lost even more time behind Super Aguri's Takuma Sato. It meant that when the double world champion emerged from the pit, he had lost the lead to Räikkönen but rejoined ahead of his teammate in second place.

This is how the 58-lap, 191.1-mile race finished, with the Finn winning his first Grand Prix driving a Ferrari in first place, some 7.2 seconds ahead of Alonso, with Hamilton producing the drive of the Australian

Grand Prix by claiming third and a podium place in his debut race. It would not have been lost on Alonso that had Sato not held up his teammate on the in-lap to the pits, he may well have finished behind him. Still, there was no doubt that the 105,000 spectators present had seen a spectacular start to the 2007 season and the birth of a new motor-racing star.

That's certainly how Niki Lauda, the former three-time world champion, saw it. 'It's quite simple,' announced the Austrian in the Albert Park paddock. 'Lewis is the best rookie I've ever seen – any time, any place, anywhere.'

The best rookie ever, in Lauda's opinion, would be embarking on a road trip around Australia with Spyker's rookie driver Adrian Sutil and Nico Rosberg of Williams before joining up with McLaren-Mercedes again in readiness for the Malaysian Grand Prix three weeks later. 'I'm very happy,' announced Hamilton after securing his first podium place with his first attempt. 'To finish third on my Formula One debut was a dream result and the end of a 14-year journey to get into the sport. The car was excellent, and I drove a good race. It was good to get that first race under my belt. The

ABOVE: Räikkönen and Fernando Alonso celebrate first and second in the Australian Grand Prix, but the real story is the rookie with a first podium in his first Formula One race.

thing is, now, after a weekend like this, the next goal is to win.'

One race old, and already Hamilton was talking about winning. Anthony Hamilton, a proud onlooker in Melbourne as his dreams for his son became reality, had his own take on Lewis's achievement. 'Formula One had better watch out,' he warned, although he had no real need to. After what had happened in Melbourne, the sport was already sitting up and taking notice.

RIGHT: Teammates rather than foes, in Australia at least, but Hamilton's already shown Alonso what he can do.

BELOW: Father and son – a proud Anthony Hamilton realises all the sacrifice and work have been worth it for this moment in Australia.

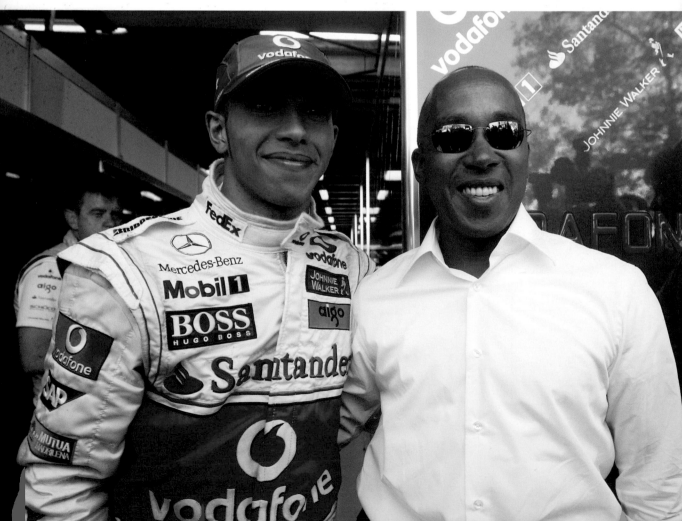

ABOVE: Hamilton's first sweet taste of podium champagne,
courtesy of Alonso in Melbourne.

RACE RESULT			
	DRIVER	**TEAM**	**POINTS**
I	Kimi Räikkönen	Ferrari	10
2	Fernando Alonso	McLaren-Mercedes	8
3	Lewis Hamilton	McLaren-Mercedes	6
4	Nick Heidfeld	BMW Sauber	5
5	Giancarlo Fisichella	Renault	4
6	Felipe Massa	Ferrari	3
7	Nico Rosberg	Williams	2
8	Ralf Schumacher	Toyota	I

CONSTRUCTORS' CHAMPIONSHIP AFTER ONE RACE		
	TEAM	**POINTS**
I	McLaren-Mercedes	14
2	Ferrari	13
3	BMW Sauber	5
4	Renault	4
5	Williams	2
6	Toyota	I

Race 2

Malaysian Grand Prix

Sepang

Sunday, 8 April 2007

Attendance: 115,000
Weather: humid, 36 °C
Track temperature: 55 °C
Number of laps: 56
Circuit length: 3.444 miles
Race distance: 192.86 miles
Fastest lap: Lewis Hamilton, 1:36.701 (lap 22)

Hamilton 2nd, 8 points (14)

SEPANG INTERNATIONAL CIRCUIT

The week before the Malaysian Grand Prix, and suitably refreshed from his road-trip exploits around Australia with his old GP2 and karting friends Nico Rosberg and Adrian Sutil, Hamilton took part in a two-day testing session at the Sepang circuit. In what was his first-ever experience of the Malaysian track, complete with dripping-sweat humidity, he managed to record a sixth-fastest time, some nine-tenths of a second behind Kimi Räikkönen, who suggested that there was much more to come from him and his Ferrari after his win in Melbourne.

'Testing was my first experience of driving in Malaysia,' Hamilton reported. 'It was tougher than I expected. The heat is incredible. I made sure I stayed hydrated.'

Between testing and returning to Malaysia for the start of the race weekend, Hamilton went to the Pacific island of Bali for some fitness training. On his return to Sepang, he tried to keep his feet on the ground: 'It was a dream start in Australia, but I'm realistic, and I know there are ups and downs in motor racing. I'm just working hard to improve all the time.'

Even so, it soon dawned on him that the sporting world had already granted him stardom. His well-chiselled looks were staring down from advertising hoardings in downtown Kuala Lumpur, and Hamilton was the centre of attention during the various media conferences that took place on the Thursday before the Grand Prix. 'It's strange,' he said. 'Unreal. Overwhelming. I still feel relaxed, but it's a new world. It's like an out-of-body experience. It's like I'm standing out there watching myself. Just yesterday, I saw this big poster of me in town. You just never believe it's real.'

Still, scrutiny had followed Hamilton throughout his career in motor sport. It was something he had grown used to dealing with: 'There's a lot of talk about expectation. There always has been. Going into that first race, there was a huge amount of expectation surrounding me. It doesn't make any difference. After Melbourne, there's clearly a possibility I can win a Grand Prix this year. As we've seen from the first race, I do have the pace. I'm here to win, whether it's this weekend or the last. As long as I get one in, that's the main thing.

ABOVE: Hot work in Sepang as Hamilton prepares for his third practice session in Malaysia.

'At the moment, I'm just trying to make sure I don't make too many mistakes. Coming into the first Grand Prix I wasn't nervous. Here in Malaysia, it's similar to every other race I've had. I have a job to do. This is a demanding circuit. Last week's testing was useful to get to know it. Now I feel very optimistic about the weekend.'

Just to make sure, though, Hamilton spent much of the Thursday night in his hotel room analysing videos of previous starts on the Sepang track. His education, he reasoned, needed furthering, and he wanted to leave nothing to chance.

Although Alonso was quickest in both of the first two Saturday qualifying sessions, it was Felipe Massa who snatched pole position on the grid in the third qualifying session when his lighter Ferrari made the most of Sepang's fast corners. Ominously for him and his team, however, Alonso recorded the day's fastest lap during the second session. Räikkönen would start in third place on the grid with Hamilton in fourth for the second successive Grand Prix after a solid qualifying performance.

To say conditions on race day were hot is something of an understatement. Down at trackside, the thermometer hit 55 °C. Even high in the stands, the 115,000 present were sweltering in temperatures touching 36 °C.

The race to the first corner was pretty hot, too. Alonso moved to the inside line and eased his way past a sleeping Massa, who gave him every opportunity to do so. It was, more or less, the only act Alonso needed to carry out to win his first race of the new season, but, in the manner of the youngest-ever double world champion, he completed it with such consummate ease.

Behind Alonso, Hamilton followed suit, passing

both Räikkönen and Massa to leapfrog into second place behind his Spanish teammate. Hamilton's manoeuvre received yet more plaudits afterwards, mainly because he had outsmarted the Ferraris – and Massa and Räikkönen were no novices – in a heavier car on what is regarded as one of the most demanding racing circuits in the world.

Massa would try and regain the advantage over his young friend from McLaren, first at turn three, when Hamilton slammed the door down the inside line, and then twice more at turn four on the sixth lap, braking too late and running wide. The second attempt cost him another place. Nick Heidfeld in his BMW Sauber made the most of Massa's loss of time in the grass to nip in ahead and relegate the Brazilian to fifth.

In his first two Formula One Grand Prix races, Hamilton had already revealed why he considered himself a racer not a driver. He followed his exciting first corner thrust in Melbourne three weeks earlier with a second equally daring manoeuvre to sweep past both the Ferraris through turns one and two. Anthony remarked later that the move was 'quintessential karting', a discipline his son had naturally excelled in, but it also revealed pure instinct and an extraordinary talent. Hamilton had no right

to pull off such a move. He was a boy amongst men, up against quicker cars and exceptional, experienced professionals. By rights, Massa should have nipped through on turn four, but it was the Brazilian who was forced into the mistake by Hamilton's perfectly timed braking. And by rights, Räikkönen should have been in second place behind Alonso. Instead, Hamilton ate them both up like candy bars. In doing so, he created a natural shield for his teammate Alonso, protecting him from both Räikkönen and Massa. It appeared to all the world to be a perfect example of teamwork in motor racing.

When Alonso dived into the pits on lap 18, having lost the use of his radio for a while, Hamilton, just as he had in Melbourne, found himself leading a Grand Prix, albeit for a couple of laps only before he too went into the pits. The lead changed hands on a regular basis over the next twenty laps as one by one the race leaders returned to the pits for a second stop. After Hamilton led for those two laps, Heidfeld took over then handed the lead back to Alonso, who moved over for Räikkönen before regaining the lead while the Finn sat in the Ferrari pits.

BELOW: Hamilton shows his mettle by holding off both Ferraris in the Malaysian Grand Prix.

ABOVE: Hamilton flashes past the grandstand tower in Malaysia.

The upshot of all these strategies was that Alonso found himself in front with 15 laps remaining, while Hamilton was in second place, some 7.17 seconds ahead of Räikkönen. This is when Hamilton gained even more credibility on the Formula One circuit. By lap 46, his lead over Räikkönen had been reduced to 5.6 seconds. By lap 55, the penultimate of the race, this had been shorn away to just 0.8 seconds. But Hamilton held on to claim the runner-up spot in the Malaysian Grand Prix, eight championship points and a second successive podium finish in his first two races in Formula One.

Those who had not taken notice after Australia now came to the party. To hold off Räikkönen in the blistering heat of Sepang with an empty drinks bottle in his car for too many laps and without making a single error was some achievement for a rookie. Nobody would have criticised the British driver if he had ended the Grand Prix in third place, with Räikkönen dividing the two McLarens. It would still have represented two back-to-back podiums and a dream start to his new career. But Hamilton wanted to go one better. By beating both Ferraris, his message was clear – even to teammate Alonso, who won the Grand Prix with a runaway 17.5-second margin, his first Formula One victory driving for his new team.

Lewis Carl Hamilton was not in Formula One to make up the numbers in the lower half of the top-eight drivers. He was already eyeing up a serious tilt at the world title.

With his face moist with sweat and his voice cracking because of emotion and effort, Hamilton was clearly drained when he gave his reaction after the race to becoming the first man since fellow Briton Peter Arundell, who twice claimed third in a Lotus in 1964, to appear on the rostrum in his opening two races. 'It was the most difficult race I've ever had,' he admitted. 'To see the two red blobs [of Ferrari] in the mirrors, knowing they were slightly lighter and quicker, is overwhelming. It was difficult

to keep them behind, and I had to dig as deep as I've ever had to.'

Staying in front of Räikkönen, as he edged ever closer to Hamilton's shiny McLaren-Mercedes in the final countdown, was especially hard. 'I can't tell you how difficult that was,' Hamilton continued, as he commented on crossing the line eight-tenths of a second ahead of his Finnish rival. 'I was sweating a lot and ran out of water. It was tricky and got hotter and hotter. In Australia, I had Fernando behind me, but he was not breathing down my neck as hard as Felipe and Kimi were today. Defending is ten times harder than trying to overtake. I wondered whether I'd be able to defend against someone like Kimi, but I could. And I'm now sitting here next to the two best drivers in the world. It's amazing. It's another step along the learning curve for me. The next one is to win. I really hope that at some point I can get that.'

Watching his son speak was Anthony, who had tried to hide his emotions behind a pair of large, dark sunglasses but had failed miserably when he had stood in the pit lane and gazed up at his son during the podium presentation. A wipe of a tear and a trembling lower lip had given the game away. 'What got to me was hearing the national anthem,' Anthony confessed. 'It had the same effect on Lewis. I was really pleased, not just for us, but for the whole country. It almost felt like the whole of Britain was patting us on the back.'

It was a pretty good day for McLaren-Mercedes in general when an exhausted Hamilton fell into the arms of race winner and teammate Alonso after stepping out of his car. Their first win in a Formula One Grand Prix since October 2005 had not been predicted in the paddock beforehand. The Ferraris were considered to be quicker, and Räikkönen was expected to carry on from where he had left off in Melbourne. Alonso and Hamilton had other ideas, however.

'Today is very important,' announced Alonso afterwards. 'It keeps motivation high, and I'm proud to have won races with two separate teams. It's amazing what we have achieved here in a very short space of time since I moved from Renault. It has taken a lot of effort from everybody.'

Räikkönen could only rue a missed opportunity. He mentioned 'too many compromises' with the car, meaning that Ferrari had erred on the side of caution because of his suspect engine, which had leaked water in Australia. 'It's a day of mixed feelings,' he said. 'We know why we were not fast enough, and we'll aim to turn the tables in Bahrain next week.'

There were other stories emanating from Malaysia that weekend. Nick Heidfeld's fourth place, ahead of Massa's Ferrari, was some achievement for the German and a result that underlined that after McLaren-Mercedes and Ferrari, BMW Sauber were next in the pecking order. Jarno Trulli brought some joy to Toyota with his seventh place, while Giancarlo Fisichella scored useful points for the second successive race. Heikki Kovalainen, Fisichella's Renault teammate, also scored his first-ever Formula One point in his first season with an eighth-place finish.

But all eyes, and all talk, were focused on another rookie. He had made the most amazing start to his Formula One career in Australia and had followed it up with an even better performance in Sepang in what would prove to be the hottest conditions of the whole 2007 season.

Nobody expected Lewis's confident surge to continue at the same pace. The two Ferrari drivers were desperate to put the young buck in his place. And the defending world champion hoped his teammate would pick away at the points, preventing the Ferraris from mounting a serious challenge to the man expected to win a third successive world title. However, as the Grand Prix circus headed for the Middle East and the Bahrain Grand Prix just seven days later, Lewis Hamilton was not prepared to read the script.

RACE RESULT			
	DRIVER	TEAM	POINTS
1	Fernando Alonso	McLaren-Mercedes	10
2	Lewis Hamilton	McLaren-Mercedes	8
3	Kimi Räikkönen	Ferrari	6
4	Nick Heidfeld	BMW Sauber	5
5	Felipe Massa	Ferrari	4
6	Giancarlo Fisichella	Renault	3
7	Jarno Trulli	Toyota	2
8	Heikki Kovalainen	Renault	1

CONSTRUCTORS' CHAMPIONSHIP AFTER TWO RACES		
	TEAM	POINTS
1	McLaren-Mercedes	32
2	Ferrari	23
3	BMW Sauber	10
4	Renault	8
5	Williams	2

DRIVERS' CHAMPIONSHIP AFTER TWO RACES		
	DRIVER	POINTS
1	Fernando Alonso	18
2	Kimi Räikkönen	16
3	Lewis Hamilton	14
4	Nick Heidfeld	10
5	Felipe Massa	7
5	Giancarlo Fisichella	7
7	Nico Rosberg	2
7	Jarno Trulli	2
9	Heikki Kovalainen	1
9	Ralf Schumacher	1

FACING PAGE (ABOVE): Räikkönen cannot get past the young rookie as they race toe to toe in Sepang.

FACING PAGE (BELOW): It's a McLaren one–two in Sepang, with the world champion and the apprentice taking first and second place at the Malaysian Grand Prix.

ABOVE: Happier days for Alonso in Sepang – the Spaniard celebrates his first win of the season, while Hamilton joins in the fun with a second place and a second successive podium finish.

Race 3

Bahrain Grand Prix

Sakhir

Sunday, 15 April 2007

Attendance: 42,000
Weather: dry/windy, 31 °C
Track temperature: 41 °C
Number of laps: 57
Circuit length: 3.363 miles
Race distance: 191.69 miles
Fastest lap: Felipe Massa, 1:34.067 (lap 42)

Hamilton 2nd, 8 points (22)

BAHRAIN INTERNATIONAL CIRCUIT

The energy-sapping humidity of Malaysia on the Sunday was swapped for the dry desert heat of Bahrain a couple of days later as the travelling circus that is Formula One upped sticks and moved across the breadth of Asia from east to west and to one of the most welcoming parties on the motor-racing circuit.

To say that Bahrain was pleased to be staging one of the seventeen Formula One Grands Prix in the season was an understatement. The Kingdom of Bahrain, and in particular His Highness, Crown Prince Shaikh Salman bin Hamad bin Isa Al Khalifa, was determined to be the focal point of Formula One in the Middle East, hence the opening of a FIA Centre of Excellence, pre-season testing, driver autograph sessions, a football tournament to coincide with testing and a Formula One street carnival in the capital Manama. No wonder opening-day attendance was up 6,000 to 22,000 and race-day attendance was a sell-out for the first time in the circuit's short history.

The weather was hot, and so was the young rookie who breezed into town having usurped nearly all the media and general-public interest. Already, after just two races, Hamilton was the man to watch. He had defied all motor-racing convention by his achievements so far on the track and appeared just as much at ease off it, where in Bahrain, a state that owns 30 per cent of McLaren, he was required to meet, greet and shake hands.

McLaren chairman Ron Dennis was not usually one to be smiling so soon into a season, but after a 2006 campaign that saw no wins for a team that has claimed more Formula One Grand Prix victories than any other during the past 25 years, even he was happy to marvel at his young acquisition. 'Lewis could have gone quicker in Malaysia, but that's not the key, is it?' he said. 'The key is to finish and get the best result you can. It's not about by how much. To keep his driving tidy and look after the car and just do what is necessary to finish second displays a level of professionalism that you would not expect to find in a guy in his second Grand Prix. These races just demonstrate to everybody his capabilities. We can all see that he is not just a capable racing driver in the car, but also very talented in his approach to the job and his physical fitness.'

If anyone doubted McLaren's decision to select

ABOVE: Pit stop – Hamilton visits the pits during qualifying in Manama.

FACING PAGE: Hamilton flanked by Ferrari's Kimi Räikkönen (left) and Felipe Massa (right) in Bahrain.

a rookie as their second driver, the results of the first two Grands Prix of the season would have put paid to that. 'The decision to appoint Lewis was not mine alone,' Dennis explained. 'In many ways, I deliberately took a slightly back seat on the process to make sure it was something supported by everybody. Of course, it was easy for me to support it, but I didn't want to find myself in a position where if he had struggled, people would be saying it was my decision. His inclusion was justified from the moment we started testing.'

At this early point in the season, all was going well at McLaren. After Ferrari's dominance during the Schumacher era, Dennis's team was back on top, and the atmosphere in an outfit that had failed to win one race during the whole of the previous year was noticeably upbeat. 'Lewis is a very good, all-round talent, but he has also got a double world champion as his teammate,' Dennis added. 'As you could see after the race in Malaysia, they were delighted for each other, and if we can maintain that team spirit through the season, we will have a great year.'

Alonso, too, was happy, at least publicly. Asked about having to cope with his young sidekick, the Spaniard had the air of an unconcerned champion.

'At the moment, I'm happy rather than worried,' he said. 'Lewis is doing a great job. He's cool and calm. He dealt with the pressure, and he kept the Ferraris behind me in Malaysia last week. Thanks to him, we were first and second.' It was difficult to believe just how much things would change in the McLaren camp in the near future.

Bernie Ecclestone was certainly happy. He had been only too well aware of the dwindling interest in the sport during the days when Michael Schumacher had turned up and won, race after race. Now there was a new kid on the block, and new fans were being introduced to Formula One as a result. 'I hope Lewis will be the next superstar of Formula One,' Ecclestone said. 'He's got all the makings. He's done an awful lot better than anybody expected him to do. He's young, good-looking and he talks to people. I wish people wouldn't keep on talking about him being coloured and all that. He doesn't need to have the praise because he happens to be coloured. And it's nothing

ABOVE: Anthony shields the heat from his son before the start of the Bahrain Grand Prix.

to do with him being good for England. He's good for Formula One. Bloody good! He's selling the business, 100 per cent.'

Hamilton, as ever, was not taking too much notice of the plaudits. He had a job to do, and this was filling up all of his attention. Besides, although excited to be racing in a Grand Prix at a circuit he had watched on television the year before, he was wary of the Ferraris. 'We need to be careful,' he warned. 'In Malaysia, we looked like we had completely closed the gap on Ferrari. I don't think that was the case at all. We got them at the first corner. If we hadn't done that, they would have gone off into the distance and won. Our overall one-lap pace is sweet. I'm not worried about that. We are quicker, but we'll have to wait and see if we are quick enough.'

He would not have to wait long. By the end of Saturday qualifying, Ferrari had let it be known that they were expecting to win in Bahrain, with Felipe Massa recording another pole position and Kimi Räikkönen claiming third. However, sandwiched between the Ferrari pair was Hamilton, who qualified on the front row of the grid for the first time in his fledgling Formula One career and in just his third race weekend. Alonso had to make do with fourth,

with the BMW Saubers of Nick Heidfeld and Robert Kubica predictably in fifth and sixth.

The day was significant, not only because Hamilton would start the race the following afternoon with a very real chance of claiming a first Grand Prix win, but also because his qualifying performance totally eclipsed his McLaren colleague Alonso. 'It's just getting better and better for me,' Hamilton announced afterwards. 'It's an amazing feeling to be on the front row in only my third race weekend. Now I want that win. I am in a really good position, but I know it is going to be a tough race.'

At least he had some experience of the Sakhir circuit, which is more than could be said for Australia and Malaysia. Back in 2004, Hamilton drove what was then his greatest race. Starting in twenty-third place in the Formula Three field, he finished eleventh in the first race, started the second race in eleventh place as a result and shot through a field of drivers that included Nico Rosberg to win in style. 'Although Formula One is obviously a bit different, I definitely feel more confident here,' he admitted. 'I am more at home with the circuit and know where you can overtake. I feel relaxed about everything, but the first corner is tricky, so we'll see what happens.'

Massa, who proved to be 0.283 seconds quicker on his final qualifying lap, would make sure turn one was more difficult, especially after the way Hamilton had shot past both Ferraris inside the first two corners in Sepang. 'I'll be a lot more aggressive this time,' the Brazilian warned. 'Now I know what Lewis can do, I won't give him as much space.'

Hamilton would be ready. 'You know what I can do at the first corner,' he responded. 'But I will have to be aware. If he needs to be more aggressive, it could be dangerous, and I want to make the first lap and score as many points as possible. I will definitely be watching out for him.'

As for seeing off teammate Alonso in qualifying, Hamilton was keen to play this down. 'I don't see beating Fernando as significant,' he insisted. 'We all have our good days and our bad days. I seem to be quite quick here and perhaps able to get more out of my runs. But give the man credit. He is a two-time world champion.'

Some people in the paddock were already making comparisons between Hamilton and Tiger Woods, such had been the young driver's impact. 'Oh, I don't take much notice of that,' was Lewis's response. 'I think Tiger is a sensational athlete, and it's an honour to be compared to him, but I'm here to do a job, and I hope I can have a similar impact on Formula One as he's had on golf.'

After the climax of the Bahrain Grand Prix, his sensational impact would become even more apparent. Unlike Malaysia, and despite everyone's concerns about turn one, there was a clean start, and Massa got away cleanly with Hamilton right behind him, while Alonso took out Räikkönen to leap into third place. Much further down the grid, however, Jenson Button, Scott Speed and David Coulthard were involved in a tangle that ended the first two drivers' participation and continued Button's miserable start for Honda. It also resulted in the safety car being used until the fourth lap, when the race resumed.

BELOW: Teamwork – the McLaren-Mercedes pit boys go to work as Hamilton waits patiently during the Bahrain Grand Prix.

In retrospect, the race may have appeared to have been a straightforward affair. After all, Massa led from the very start to record his first win of the season. But Hamilton could, and possibly should, have notched up his first-ever win as a Formula One driver. He certainly gave it his all, recording fastest laps on the eighth, ninth, fifteenth, seventeenth and eighteenth laps and proving to be the quickest in the final phase of the race. What cost him the winner's place was the second stint of the Grand Prix when performance appeared to drain from the car, the blame later being laid on the used tyres which were put into use after he pitted during lap 19.

Räikkönen threatened at one time to challenge Hamilton for second place, while Alonso had a disappointing day, finishing fifth – having led on the twenty-first lap when the leaders visited the pits – after being passed by Heidfeld on the thirty-second lap. At the end of the race, it was obvious that Hamilton was catching Massa fast, but the chequered flag came to the Brazilian's rescue after his lead had been whittled down to just 2.3 seconds.

ABOVE: Look behind you! Hamilton keeps Räikkönen at bay during the Bahrain Grand Prix.

Once again, everyone turned to the record books. By recording three podium finishes (third, second and now second again) in his first three races, Hamilton became the first Formula One driver to do so, even eclipsing such greats of the sport as Michael Schumacher and Juan Manuel Fangio. The eight points snapped up in Bahrain also meant that, with twenty-two points to his name, he now shared the lead in the drivers' championship alongside Räikkönen

and Alonso, with the latter, his teammate and double world champion, having been soundly beaten all weekend by the rookie.

'I think it's a fantastic achievement, and I'm extremely proud,' Hamilton announced afterwards. 'I'm now looking forward to Silverstone and the British Grand Prix in July and seeing how many fans there are. I've not been back for five weeks. I hope I'll still be able to walk the streets.'

He was so happy with his achievement that in the post-race media conference he goaded his friend Massa, who was happy to play along. 'Ten laps more and I would have given you a race,' he told the winner of the Grand Prix.

'Yeah, but I was taking it easy,' Massa replied. 'I was saving the car.'

The McLaren camp was understandably ecstatic. 'Three races to be a contender for the world championship is phenomenal,' said Martin Whitmarsh, the team's chief executive. 'We all have to conclude now that Lewis is a serious title challenger. He'll want to go better now and win a race. I don't think anyone doubts that he'll do that this season.'

Certainly not Sir Jackie Stewart, who was fast becoming Hamilton's greatest admirer from the list of former greats. 'It's not inconceivable that Lewis could win the world title this year,' was his response after witnessing Bahrain first hand. 'McLaren are clearly the team to beat. If Lewis doesn't win it this year, then he is certain to do so in the next three.'

Nigel Mansell was a little more cautious. 'Lewis is driving for one of the best teams in the world at the present time with a competitive car, but, nevertheless, he's been able to accomplish more in a shorter space of time than any driver I've ever seen,' said the British former world champion. 'He's lucked into a fabulous car. What he's done has been very impressive, but it's what he should have been doing anyway.'

One of the happiest men on the grid that Sunday evening in the Middle East was Hamilton's father. 'It was crazy getting his first podium, crazier getting second in Malaysia and then leading the championship with Fernando Alonso and Kimi Räikkönen at the same time,' said Anthony. 'You couldn't write it. There's a lot said in Formula One about young drivers not being able to cut the mustard. Well, hopefully, we've done some good for some other young drivers who are good enough to sit in the seat.'

LEWIS HAMILTON

Ron Dennis was also delighted by the way his two drivers were approaching the championship. 'We're privileged to have the double world champion in the car, and the chemistry between the two is fantastic,' he announced. 'Fernando and Lewis are passionate people, different characters, and it's very easy to work with them. There isn't an issue between them, and we'll make sure it stays that way. We want to win the world championship. We have the young pretender and the champion, and we owe it to them to give them equal opportunity.'

Alonso, for his part, appeared relaxed about his disappointing weekend. 'Finishing fifth is not a drama,' he said. 'I am leading the world championship with others after the third race, and we could only have dreamt of that before the start of the season with the performances of Ferrari in testing. This was not a great race for me, but these things happen.'

Next up for Alonso would be the Spanish Grand Prix, his home race and the ideal chance to restate his position as the main man in Formula One. To do so would mean putting the young upstart Hamilton, teammate or not, in his place.

For all his proud statements, though, and despite the happy position his drivers and team found themselves in after three races, Ron Dennis sensed the very first seeds of trouble that would decimate the season later in the year. 'The first three questions to the drivers after the race went to Lewis,' he recalled. 'I could just sense Fernando thinking, "Hang on, I'm the double world champion here."'

Maybe, but it was Lewis Hamilton making all the news.

RACE RESULT			
	DRIVER	TEAM	POINTS
1	Felipe Massa	Ferrari	10
2	Lewis Hamilton	McLaren-Mercedes	8
3	Kimi Räikkönen	Ferrari	6
4	Nick Heidfeld	BMW Sauber	5
5	Fernando Alonso	McLaren-Mercedes	4
6	Robert Kubica	BMW Sauber	3
7	Jarno Trulli	Toyota	2
8	Giancarlo Fisichella	Renault	1

DRIVERS' CHAMPIONSHIP AFTER THREE RACES		
	DRIVER	POINTS
1	Fernando Alonso	22
1	Kimi Räikkönen	22
1	Lewis Hamilton	22
4	Felipe Massa	17
5	Nick Heidfeld	15
6	Giancarlo Fisichella	8
7	Jarno Trulli	4
8	Robert Kubica	3
9	Nico Rosberg	2
10	Heikki Kovalainen	1
11	Ralf Schumacher	1

CONSTRUCTORS' CHAMPIONSHIP AFTER THREE RACES		
	TEAM	POINTS
1	McLaren-Mercedes	44
2	Ferrari	39
3	BMW Sauber	18
4	Renault	9
5	Toyota	5
6	Williams	2

FACING PAGE: Another second place for Hamilton – a wave to the crowd and a third successive podium, this time in Bahrain.

Race 4

Spanish Grand Prix

Barcelona

Sunday, 13 May 2007

Attendance: 140,000
Weather: sunny, 29 °C
Track temperature: 50 °C
Number of laps: 65
Circuit length: 2.892 miles
Race distance: 187.98 miles
Fastest lap: Felipe Massa, 1:22.68 (lap 14)

Hamilton 2nd, 8 points (30)

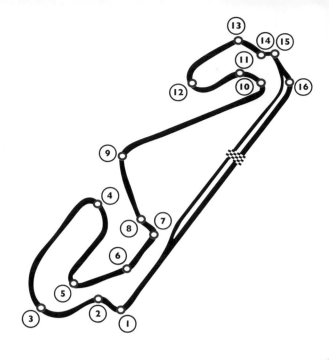

CIRCUIT DE CATALUNYA

It had taken just three races for the world to sit up and take notice of the new kid in the Formula One class. Hamilton, the first driver to finish on the podium in each of his first three races, had received some plaudits even before the start of his inaugural season, but this was nothing compared with the days before the Spanish Grand Prix when the circus first touched down in Europe.

The chief admirer turned out to be Niki Lauda, who had already predicted great things from the Hertfordshire driver on the eve of the first Grand Prix in Australia. After three races, the former three-time world champion had seen enough. 'As unbelievable as it sounds, at the moment I can see Hamilton heading the drivers' rankings,' announced the popular Austrian. 'This is because he is young, his experience is clean and he is as fast as Alonso. I did not expect a rookie to be so advanced and strong-minded as he is. If his learning curve continues to go upwards, we can expect even more from him. If the team are able to improve the performance and create an advantage over Ferrari, this year's championship will be a duel between him and Alonso.'

Unsurprisingly, Michael Schumacher, who had an advisory role with Ferrari, was a little less forthcoming on his first return to a Grand Prix circuit since his retirement at the end of the previous season, but even the former seven-time world champion was impressed by what he had seen so far. 'Hamilton is doing a very good job,' said the 38-year-old German. 'It's not a surprise to me after seeing his races last year in GP2. But maybe it's a surprise that he can deliver it so consistently. There you go. He is well prepared, he is quick and he does the job.'

Perhaps Schumacher was happy his own career had come to an end, especially with the emergence of Hamilton on the grid. He would not say as much, of course, but suddenly a new life playing football, being part of the Team New Zealand America's Cup team and mucking out his wife's stables seemed preferable to the possibility of being beaten by a 22-year-old rookie.

Already, after just three races, talk was growing of a very real rivalry between the two McLaren drivers. Ron Dennis admitted to having what he described as a 'paternal' chat with Alonso, fearing his £15-million-a-year driver was less than comfortable with all the growing hysteria surrounding Hamilton. The British

ABOVE: The yellow helmet – it must be Hamilton as he practises at the Circuit de Catalunya.

driver, after three consecutive podiums, had gained sufficient confidence to start talking about winning, too. 'I'm here to win, not finish second,' was his statement on arriving at the Circuit de Catalunya. A win would be a maiden victory in Formula One for the rookie, and it would be achieved at Alonso's home circuit, in front of a huge and largely partisan crowd in favour of the Spaniard.

'Fernando's the toughest driver I've competed against, and it's hard to beat him, but it doesn't mean I can't,' Hamilton continued. 'I'm free to do what I want. I never go to a race with expectations. I go with a target. That is to be at the front, and the ultimate aim is to win, which is the mentality I've always gone racing with. You have to have the belief that you can succeed in order to ensure you have the commitment. That is true for anything in any walk of life.'

Although he sounded like an experienced Formula One driver, Hamilton was prepared to admit that things had gone better than expected. 'Anyone in my position would be surprised,' he admitted. 'I've been in the right place at the right time and done a good job. I think I've had luck on my side. It's pretty cool when you're the first rookie to do something. Ten years ago, I couldn't have imagined being here, and now I'm here with the best drivers in the world. It's going to help me driving in Europe for the next few races. I feel more confident on a track where I've raced before. I'll feel a bit more relaxed, a bit more at home. Previous experience will be a boost to my confidence.'

The belief in the paddock was that Alonso, normally so cool and collected, had been rattled by the emergence of the new young star. This was not supposed to happen, at least not in the Spaniard's own script. The double world champion had left Ferrari to try and claim a third, back-to-back world title, but this time with a new team. He was number one, even if McLaren had always had a policy of having no favoured drivers in their team. This new kid was supposed to watch and learn, take a healthy smattering of points, fend off would-be challengers to Alonso and admire his teammate becoming world champion for a third time. Instead, Hamilton had had the temerity to sit alongside him at the top of the drivers' table.

There were some observers who argued that this unexpected challenge to Alonso's dominance had started to get to the world champion's driving. Sir Jackie Stewart, having watched Alonso practise at his home Grand Prix, was one. 'He missed the apex of one turn completely this morning,' said the Scottish icon. 'He made three big mistakes. Alonso was over-driving. After the first mistake, he should have backed off. Instead, he compounded it by carrying on. Usually, he is so smooth. I don't think there is any question that Alonso is feeling it. Hamilton's brilliant start has definitely given him something to think about.'

At testing the week before, Ferrari had dominated the times so much that Honda's Jenson Button referred to them as 'stupidly fast'. On the Friday of the Spanish Grand Prix, however, Alonso set the fastest time in practice. The Spaniard, like all good champions, had assigned what had happened in Bahrain to history. That was then, and this was now. Barcelona was his Grand Prix, and he wanted to ensure everything went according to plan.

The Saturday was not quite as successful for Alonso, nor for Hamilton, although in the latter's case qualifying on the front two rows of the grid for the fourth successive Grand Prix could hardly be considered a failure in only his fourth race. Ferrari's Felipe Massa took pole for the third consecutive

BELOW: An interested observer – the great Michael Schumacher, in the pits in Spain, wonders whether Hamilton will one day take his records.

ABOVE: A close team – Hamilton laughs with his mechanics in Spain.

BELOW: A study in concentration – Hamilton, deep in thought, slips his balaclava on.

time – his fifth pole in the last six races – in front of the watching Michael Schumacher. Alonso was alongside him on the front row of the grid, just three-hundredths of a second slower. Kimi Räikkönen and Hamilton took up positions three and four. Hamilton was fastest in two of the practice sessions but ended up 0.3 seconds behind Massa in final qualifying.

'I am very motivated and confident about the race,' said Massa afterwards. 'I hope the spectators see a real spectacle tomorrow and I make the most of being in pole. Everybody is really pushing hard, though. When you have competition so high between all these four drivers, you cannot say which is the most dangerous to your aspirations. Everyone seems to be doing a very good job, and you need to be aware of all of them.'

His Ferrari teammate Räikkönen, joint leader of the championship with Alonso and Hamilton, was also speaking in confident terms. 'My feel for the car is rapidly improving,' he announced.

Alonso, meanwhile, was predicting a furious shoot-out at the Circuit de Catalunya. 'Anybody in the top four is capable of winning this race,' announced the world champion. That said, he was confident in the progress he and his team had made, and of his chances of winning in Spain. 'When I joined McLaren, I expected that I might spend the first five months waiting for a good car,' he explained. 'But I have been very pleased with the work we have done and how strong our car is. From what we saw all weekend, it performed really well, we were quick in all the practice sessions and the first two qualifying sessions, and it is close with Felipe, so I have to be confident.'

Hamilton was also approaching Sunday's race with high expectations. 'I believe that I have a strong race strategy,' he said. 'Anything is possible from the second row, and we have been quick throughout the weekend. I've started from fourth on a number of occasions now, so I have an idea what to do.' He did admit, however, to feeling the strains of almost overnight fame. His home in Tewin, Hertfordshire, where he lived with father Anthony, step-mother Linda and brother Nicholas, was almost permanently besieged by paparazzi. 'I've felt like a prisoner inside my own home,' he admitted. 'To see so many photographers parked outside my house has been the weirdest thing. They are there from eight in the morning until six at night, just sitting in their cars.'

A report in May revealed that a preliminary poll for the BBC Sports Personality of the Year award had

ABOVE: Turn one in Spain, and it's Felipe Massa (left) versus Fernando Alonso (right).

44 per cent of people picking Hamilton, way ahead of tennis star Andy Murray (23 per cent) and Welsh boxer Joe Calzaghe (14 per cent). Hamilton, understandably, was finding it difficult to take in his sudden celebrity status. 'You couldn't imagine how I feel,' he explained. 'I'm walking down the paddock as a normal person and everyone sees me as this big Formula One driver. It's very strange. The truth is, I feel exactly the same person that I was in 2006, or before that. I'm now a Formula One driver, but it hasn't fully sunk in yet. It's hard to absorb what I've done.

'I used to come into the McLaren Communications Centre at races to have lunch and say hello to everyone. Now I have my own room. I've taken over Kimi's place. It's really weird, like sitting here watching myself race. I know how to keep my feet on the ground, though.'

Which is precisely what McLaren boss Ron Dennis expected to hear. 'Lewis's approach is confident but devoid of arrogance,' Dennis explained. 'I hope we can maintain an environment that means he doesn't change.'

Despite this, more Formula One luminaries were offering their glowing verdicts on the rookie. 'I'm trying to keep some objectivity, but it's impossible to avoid the most extreme of superlatives when describing Lewis,' admitted Murray Walker, the veteran voice of British motor sport. 'In my experience, no one has been as good so quickly in Formula One as Lewis. From what I can tell, I don't see Lewis being affected by outside, glamorous influences. It's too fanciful to expect Lewis to remain in contention for the championship throughout the year.' Fanciful, yes, but as Hamilton would go on to prove, not impossible.

Not for the first time, the Spanish Grand Prix would be shaped by what went on at the first corner. It was Alonso who made the better start of the two drivers on the front row of the grid. As they careered towards the first turn, the Spaniard was up alongside Massa when their two cars touched. This forced Alonso to veer off the track into the grass, and by the time he had rejoined both Hamilton and Räikkönen had surged ahead, with the young British driver jumping from fourth to second as a result.

Once again, Hamilton had revealed his unnerving ability to make an emphatic start. He had already nudged ahead of Räikkönen into third place before the bonus of seeing the front two collide. As the cars sped on to turn two, with barely ten seconds of the race completed, Hamilton had already jumped two places and was sitting right behind the leader. More luck would befall him and his McLaren team when Räikkönen retired from the race with an electrical problem on the ninth lap, and when both Massa and Alonso dived into the pits ten laps later Hamilton once again found himself leading a Formula One Grand Prix. This initial lead would last just three laps before Hamilton refuelled, and although the rookie would lead from the forty-third to forty-seventh laps, following Massa's second trip to the pits, Hamilton's second stint of refuelling let Massa return to the front of the race with eighteen laps remaining.

To Hamilton's credit, he did not sit back and accept second place. Massa led his challenger by 10.5 seconds on lap 48. As the Brazilian crossed the finish line to receive the chequered flag after 65 laps, the lead had been whittled down to 6.7 seconds. Alonso was disappointed to trail home third in front of a partisan Spanish crowd numbering 140,000, with the cool Polish rookie Robert Kubica claiming fourth in a BMW Sauber, David Coulthard, proving there was still much life left in the oldest driver on the grid, securing fifth place in his Red Bull and Nico Rosberg, impressing again, finishing sixth driving his Williams.

Once again, Hamilton had rewritten the record books, something he appeared to be achieving after every single race. At twenty-two years, four months and six days old, he found himself leading the world championship, becoming the youngest-ever driver to achieve this mark. Ironically, he usurped the man who had launched the team Hamilton was now driving for, the late Bruce McLaren, who had achieved the same distinction back in 1962. Hamilton's second place

– his third runner-up spot in a row – lifted him two points ahead of teammate Alonso at the top of the drivers' championship and meant that he had claimed four podium places in his first four races, which was another record in the history of the sport.

Afterwards, confidence exuded from the young, and extremely happy, Englishman. When he was asked if he felt at any point in the race he could actually have won, he replied, 'Yes, from the first corner to the chequered flag. I never stopped pushing.' His actions immediately after the race told their own story, too. As he and Massa came to the weighing room, Hamilton made a point of congratulating the race winner by patting him on the back and adding some quiet but interesting words. 'Get you next time,' he promised the Brazilian. He wasn't joking.

Four races had been completed, and Hamilton's sensational arrival onto the Formula One scene appeared, if this was possible, to be gathering pace. 'I keep saying I'm living the dream,' he said afterwards. 'It's so true. To come into my fourth Grand Prix and come out of it leading the championship is just incredible. I could not be happier. I came into the season with an open mind but never felt this was possible. I just hoped I would come in and do a good job. I have been working so many years for this. The whole thing is getting bigger and bigger.'

If there were those who suddenly started believing Hamilton could achieve the unthinkable and actually become world champion in his first year, the driver had news for them. He had reached this conclusion the race before. 'Even from the last race, we felt there was a possibility I can win the title,' he revealed. 'We have to be realistic, though. This is my first season. There will be ups and downs. As long as the team keeps the reliability and I can keep the mistakes down to a minimum, then we have a chance.

'Going into this race, we knew we had a good strategy. At this track, you can't overtake. The aim was to gain as many places in the first corner as possible. I got past Kimi. Fernando went off and almost hit me when he came back. We didn't quite have the pace of Felipe, but, as I said to him, we'll get him soon.'

His McLaren teammate was not quite as happy. Alonso had to make to do with third and see the lead he had jointly held with Hamilton in the

FACING PAGE: The pain in Spain – an over-aggressive Alonso comes off second best to Hamilton at the Spanish Grand Prix.

drivers' championship disappear as a result. He laid the blame for this squarely on the shoulders of the uncompromising Massa after the incident at turn one. 'I was in front at the first corner, almost half a length in front,' the Spaniard insisted. 'Unfortunately, he did not think so, and we touched. In 99 per cent of incidents like this, both cars finish the race at the first corner. When you are fighting for the championship, doing something like that is a very risky thing to do. We were lucky to finish. My car was damaged and was more difficult to drive as a result. We needed a miracle after that. I am very disappointed. I was three-hundredths of a second off pole and leading the race at the first corner. At the second, I was off. Five hundred metres into the race, it changed completely.'

Massa, with some justification, adopted a different viewpoint. 'I didn't do anything wrong,' he insisted. 'When I have made mistakes in the past, I have always said so. Come on. This is racing. It was tight. I was inside and went for it. It was a risk for both of us. The first corner is important. You don't want to lose like I did in Malaysia. We touched. Fernando was trying to push me inside. It was a small contact, but for me a normal incident.' Besides, he wasn't going to let a spat with Alonso spoil his day, a win and the fact that he had edged to within three points of leader Hamilton in the drivers' championship. 'Fantastic!' he added. 'I can't find the words to describe the emotions I feel after such a closely fought race.'

The last word, though, had to belong to Hamilton as he looked ahead to race five in the Formula One calendar, the jewel in the sport's crown – the Monaco Grand Prix. 'I'm going to be gunning for the win in Monaco,' he promised.

After a Spanish Grand Prix that saw him top the drivers' leaderboard, who could doubt him.

RACE RESULT			
	DRIVER	TEAM	POINTS
1	Felipe Massa	Ferrari	10
2	Lewis Hamilton	McLaren-Mercedes	8
3	Fernando Alonso	McLaren-Mercedes	6
4	Robert Kubica	BMW Sauber	5
5	David Coulthard	Red Bull	4
6	Nico Rosberg	Williams	3
7	Heikki Kovalainen	Renault	2
8	Takuma Sato	Super Aguri	1

DRIVERS' CHAMPIONSHIP AFTER FOUR RACES		
	DRIVER	POINTS
1	Lewis Hamilton	30
2	Fernando Alonso	28
3	Felipe Massa	27
4	Kimi Räikkönen	22
5	Nick Heidfeld	15
6	Robert Kubica	8
6	Giancarlo Fisichella	8
8	Nico Rosberg	5
9	David Coulthard	4
9	Jarno Trulli	4
11	Heikki Kovalainen	3
12	Takuma Sato	1
12	Ralf Schumacher	1

CONSTRUCTORS' CHAMPIONSHIP AFTER FOUR RACES		
	TEAM	POINTS
1	McLaren-Mercedes	58
2	Ferrari	49
3	BMW Sauber	23
4	Renault	11
5	Williams	5
5	Toyota	5
7	Red Bull	4
8	Super Aguri	1

FACING PAGE: Here we go again! Hamilton sprays the podium champagne in Spain.

Race 5

Monaco Grand Prix

Monte Carlo

Sunday, 27 May 2007

Attendance: 120,000
Weather: sunny, 24 °C
Track temperature: 35 °C
Number of laps: 78
Circuit length: 2.075 miles
Race distance: 161.85 miles
Fastest lap: Fernando Alonso, 1:15.284 (lap 44)

Hamilton 2nd, 8 points (38)

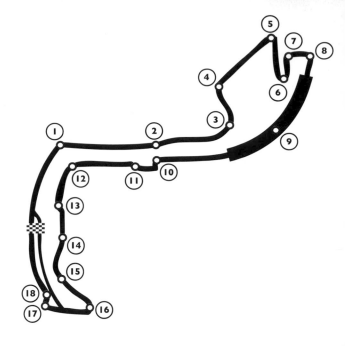

CIRCUIT DE MONACO

Sir Jackie Stewart knows a thing or two about motor racing – and racing drivers, for that matter. Of all the great British drivers – Stirling Moss, Jim Clark, Graham Hill, Nigel Mansell – only Stewart had become world champion on three separate occasions. The Scot was not one to hand out plaudits easily, but he was prepared to make an exception in the case of Lewis Hamilton.

He had already suggested that Hamilton could become a major star at the start of the season, but, having seen him take pole position in the drivers' championship, Stewart revealed to the world his true thoughts, explaining that he'd asked the rookie to be his guest at the Springfield Club the previous December. The club can be found in Hackney in London's East End. Stewart is president and proud of his work trying to keep kids from single-parent families living in social housing in east London away from the life of crime that so many of their contemporaries choose. Every Christmas, he invites a famous contact of his to come to the club; however, in 2006 he decided to ask a young man with little fame but the ability, he guessed, to identify with the youths.

'This is a troubled area, with nine gangs who shoot people,' Stewart explained. 'Lewis is the kind of guy who shows kids that if they think a little differently, they don't have to go down this route. He presented trophies, mixed with everyone and made them feel at home. Senna, Mansell, Hill, they've all been there, but Lewis was the best guest ever.

'That, for me, was a sign of what was to come. I knew he had won in every class and was a very good driver, but this was something different. I think Lewis is going to rewrite the book. We're going to see a new generation of what I call properly prepared professional racing drivers. Lewis will set the benchmark for them all. I don't think there has been anyone like that. Michael Schumacher became one, but I'm talking about being fully rounded, about the whole package. Lewis has the mind for it, the attitude, the God-given skill, but he's already recognising that he needs something else. That's why he's in the factory every day. That's why he is already more popular than many British drivers who have won world titles. And he is doing it with style and humility. The boy has excellent balance. Niki Lauda and James Hunt changed the culture of racing

ABOVE: Hamilton receives instructions as he waits for his turn during the third practice session at Monaco.

Rosberg, the son of the former world champion Keke, is a year younger. 'When Lewis came to Italy, which was then the centre of karting, I thought, "Who the hell is this guy?" He soon proved himself, though, and Robert, Lewis and I were always fighting for the victories. We shared a mutual respect. We are all very determined people.'

At the other end of the scale, Gerhard Berger, the Austrian veteran of 210 Grands Prix, argued that having McLaren boss Ron Dennis as his mentor and benefactor for the past dozen years could have softened Hamilton's resolve. 'I saw how Lewis had been spoiled, never had to fight for a drive, how everything was organised for him, and I wondered how he could have a killer instinct in a Formula One car,' he explained. 'Well, like everyone, Lewis has made a fantastic impression on me.'

The glitz and the glamour of Monte Carlo is, of course, a different world from the Springfield Club in Hackney, but it was here, on the Côte d'Azure, that Lewis Hamilton soon became the star. Nico Rosberg, for one, was predicting great things for his friend in the principality. 'Lewis has won other races in Monaco, so driving a Formula One car round the streets will not be a problem for him,' he said. 'Everything happens a bit faster, but it's still a racing car, not a rocket ship. Lewis will be very competitive in Monaco, just as he has been everywhere else this season.'

The world's most valuable piece of jewellery attempted to usurp Hamilton when the pair both appeared on the deck of *The Floridian*, one of the larger, more exquisite yachts moored in the harbour in Monte Carlo. The Ponahalo diamond was unveiled on the Thursday before the Grand Prix, but it was Hamilton who gained all the attention, and a fair few diamonds himself. The gems were inlaid along the side of his helmet, spelling the words 'Monaco 07'. He was also presented with a jewel-encrusted ring, part of the promotion that is laid on annually in Monaco by the diamond traders Steinmetz.

Hamilton was delighted with his new look. 'I'm blinged up,' he announced, jokingly. 'I've bling on my helmet. How cool is that? And I've even got a ring that spins.' The gems were an omen as well. McLaren are the most successful team at the Monaco Grand Prix, with 13 victories since the race began back in 1929, and their last win took place in 2005 when Kimi Räikkönen also wore diamonds on his helmet.

Hamilton was not counting his chickens because

drivers. They, basically, didn't give a damn. But Lewis can become the role model. There are twenty-two drivers on the grid and, of those, only six are any good. Out of those, only three are extraordinary talents, and out of those there is usually one genius. I think that genius is Lewis Hamilton.'

More and more famous figures from the world of motor sport, both new and old, were prepared to eulogise on Hamilton's account. Robert Kubica and Nico Rosberg pretty much had European karting at their mercy until Hamilton came along, and the pair had been racing against the British driver ever since. 'Lewis is the hardest driver I've ever met in my career before coming into Formula One,' said Kubica, at 22 the same age as Hamilton. 'We had many nice moments and many fights but always with fair play.'

of that, however. 'I'm not really a superstitious person,' he said. 'I don't know if that's going to have an impact on how well I do. But what I will say is that Monaco is the best circuit of the year. There is nowhere like it for getting the adrenalin going, because the track is so tight and there are no run-off areas. There is no room for errors, and that makes it all the more exciting for a driver.

'I have always run well at Monaco. I am here with the intention of fighting for a win, but that's always the case. I feel very comfortable going into the weekend. The team have done a great job, I'm fit – probably fitter than I've been all season – and I'm also more relaxed than at any time in the season. I'm expecting it to go well. I just need to make sure I'm focused. You need to be calm and enjoy the atmosphere but do the job.'

Rumours were beginning to spread about growing unrest in the McLaren camp. For sure, Alonso had not come to McLaren to be upstaged by a rookie, and there were suggestions that the double world champion and his entourage were growing increasingly unhappy with what they perceived to be a bias in the team towards the Englishman. Alonso attempted to play this down on the eve of first practice. 'I'm not reading too much into these rumours,' he insisted. 'People saying such things is normal in Formula One. If you do well for two or three races, they say the championship is over. If you have two or three bad results, then the championship's over for you. The truth is that there are 17 races in the season, and I'm hoping to go into the final race with a possibility of winning the title once more.'

Hamilton, though, also planned to be there at the end. 'I don't see why not,' he proclaimed. 'We just need to remain consistent, but it's been an amazing journey so far.' This journey would take a twist the following day in free practice.

Despite Hamilton's familiarity with the streets of Monaco, he still managed to crash into a tyre wall at 100 mph after losing control coming out of a 170-mph straight and into the Sainte Devote corner. The young driver walked away unscathed, although team doctor Aki Hintsa still gave him the once-over on his return to the garage.

'Everyone makes mistakes, and I'm only human,' was Hamilton's response after the shock of actually

BELOW: Bling boy – Hamilton's diamond-studded helmet in Monaco.

making an error. 'I was pushing and right on the limit, which is something you have to do at Monaco. I just locked the rear wheels, and, as it came before the apex, I lost the back end, tried to brake too quick and went off into the wall. There is no room for error in the streets here. You learn something new every day, and I've learned how not to put the car into a barrier. These things happen, but we're extremely quick, we made some good set-up changes and we're looking very competitive for Saturday.' Asked how he would respond to the crash in the next day's qualifying, Hamilton's answer brimmed with confidence. 'I'm ready to go faster,' he announced.

Nobody seemed too concerned about the setback, not even team boss Ron Dennis. 'It was a mistake that all drivers of all standards make,' was his view on the incident. 'I'd rather this in practice than in qualifying or in the race. Monaco is a big challenge for everyone, and I think he's got a few brownie points left.'

Even before qualifying, the talk in the paddock was of a prospective first Formula One Grand Prix win for Hamilton, and where better to pull it off than Monaco? Nobody in the sport had ever won in the principality on their first effort, but Hamilton had never lost there,

having won both his races around the streets in Formula Three and also the year before in GP2.

'Driving around here is every driver's dream,' he insisted. 'I love this track and the atmosphere. It's a beautiful place. It's amazing coming here knowing that years ago I watched Ayrton [Senna] and Michael [Schumacher] win here. It's the race we all want to win, and I used to dream that one day it would be me winning here.'

Jackie Stewart, a three-time Monaco winner, could be found eulogising yet again over his favourite subject – Lewis Hamilton – after witnessing his practice sessions. 'If my fairy godmother could wave a magic wand and grant me one more race – and say I could win it at that – this would be it,' he explained, resplendent in his tartan cap and trousers. 'Lewis has that chance. It helps that he's in a McLaren and has Ron Dennis's blessing, but when he climbs into the car all the wisdom that has been passed on to him is of little consequence. The car is entirely in his hands from that moment. It's a matter of how capable he is of removing emotion from his mind. I believe he does that well already, but it's crucial because Monaco is all about not making mistakes. It's about being focused and keeping your mental discipline. I'm enormously impressed by the guy.'

So, too, it seemed, were arch rivals Ferrari, or at least their boss Jean Todt. 'Lewis is very skilled and talented,' said the Frenchman. 'He has a good car, he has a good team and he is a great driver, so I'm full of respect for this guy.'

Todt knew that he and his team would be in for a hard time the next day when the McLaren drivers claimed both places on the front row of the grid, with Alonso in pole and Hamilton alongside him in second. Massa had to make do with third and Räikkönen a disastrous sixteenth after the Finn bounced his car over a kerb exiting the Swimming Pool corner, damaging its rear suspension in the process.

For a time, Hamilton even thought he might claim his first pole in his still embryonic Formula One career, but Alonso, showing impeccable timing, bettered his fastest lap by two-tenths of a second with just eleven seconds remaining of a frenetic qualifying session. Hamilton might well have pipped his Spanish teammate, but he was baulked by Mark Webber's Red Bull. 'I lost half a second, but that's racing,' he said, before adding, somewhat mischievously, 'I don't

know whether Webber didn't see me, but he said in the drivers' briefing that we need to be hard on people who hold others up, then he came out and held me up.'

The truth was that he was delighted to be starting his first-ever Monaco Grand Prix in second place, and, with rain showers forecast for the race, he reckoned he could conjure up a stiff challenge to Alonso. 'If I get a better start and it looks as if I can pass Fernando, I will,' he promised, which would prove to be an ironic statement. 'I'm sure the team will speak to both of us before the race, and I won't do anything silly. I feel good about our strategy, and I think we can come away with a one–two. I think it will be really interesting to see what happens tomorrow.'

Twenty-four hours later and the 2007 season turned controversial. It would involve the McLaren-Mercedes team and would reveal the first signs of enmity between their two drivers. McLaren achieved their cherished one–two, with Alonso securing the team's 150th Grand Prix win in Formula One. The team nudged further ahead in the constructors' championship, and Alonso drew level with Hamilton at the top of the drivers' championship with 38 points, but neither looked like celebrating afterwards.

BELOW: The face of Ferrari – team principal Jean Todt looks on during qualifying at Monaco.

LEWIS HAMILTON

Under normal circumstances, another runner-up spot – his fourth in succession – and at the most glamorous race in the whole season would be a cause for joy, but Hamilton's customary smile witnessed after the first four races in the calendar had been transformed into a glower after the fifth. The reason was simple. Team boss Dennis had ordered his rookie driver to stay in second place as early as the twentieth lap out of 78 and not risk causing a crash involving both McLaren cars by attempting to overtake race leader Alonso, who used his favourable pole position to ensure he led the 22 drivers as they careered towards the first turn on the street circuit. This was entirely against Hamilton's natural racing instincts, and it clearly showed.

McLaren's policy had been decided even before the start of the race. Hamilton carried a heavier load of fuel going into the last section of qualifying, which meant that he would be handicapped in the race for pole. In no other race is pole more important than Monaco, where the cramped streets make overtaking close to impossible. Then Hamilton was called in twice during the race to be refuelled earlier than had

been planned, denying the British driver the chance to hurtle around the streets when his lighter load would have recorded faster laps. Finally, to add insult to injury, he received instructions over his radio after less than a third of the race not to overtake Alonso when he was just a second behind him. He would finish second, a staggering 69 seconds ahead of third-placed Massa. Räikkönen, the only other potential challenger to McLaren's quest for the drivers' title, did well to surge up the field from sixteenth to finish eighth, especially at a circuit such as Monaco. Once again, he frustrated Ferrari by revealing that he was the quickest driver on the circuit, but Saturday's qualifying did for his chances of winning.

Perhaps Hamilton's best achievement during the Monaco weekend was that he managed, just, to keep his true thoughts to himself when the inquests began after the race. 'I have the number two on my car, so I'm the number-two driver,' he said, quite obviously angry at the events that had just unfolded. 'At the end of the day, I am a rookie coming into my first

BELOW: Controversy in the principality – Alonso wins, but Hamilton is told to stay second.

ABOVE: Mixed emotions for Hamilton – second place in his first Formula One Monaco Grand Prix, but the rookie believed he was prevented from winning.

season, so I can't complain about finishing second in my first Monaco Grand Prix. I can see that I'm on a similar track to Fernando, which is positive. It's just something I'll have to live with.'

Even Ron Dennis, who made the decision to hold back his prodigy, was uncomfortable with his own actions. 'We are pleased with the one–two, but my job carries difficult decisions,' he admitted. 'There are many things that are unique at Monte Carlo. A lot of people in England will feel there is some favouritism or penalty given to Lewis, but we are scrupulously fair at all times in the Grand Prix team. This circuit has to be addressed, though, which is why we've won here 14 times.

'I make no excuses for instructing the drivers to slow their pace after the first stop and to affect our strategy based on the possibility of other cars affecting us if

the safety car was deployed. I don't like to slow drivers down, and I don't like frustrating them, because I'm an absolute racer, but it is the way you have to win the Monaco Grand Prix.

'I think Lewis is understandably frustrated and disappointed. There will be a place where he is absolutely free to race, but this is not one of them. I don't feel good about it, but we're the ones ahead in the championship, and that is my job. I have been monstrously criticised in the past for frittering away the opportunity of a world championship by not favouring a driver. We will never favour one driver. This was a unique one-off.'

Alonso was clearly not embarrassed by being presented with the victory on a plate. 'It has been a fantastic weekend,' he declared. 'To do the hat-trick of pole, setting the fastest lap and winning is something special, even more so here in Monaco. It was fabulous to win again, and it was the easiest and nicest victory so far.'

Too easy, according to some, including the FIA, the sport's governing body, which decided it would sit in judgement over the affair. Team orders were, after all, banned following the infamous Austrian Grand Prix in 2001 when Rubens Barrichello was ordered to make way for his Ferrari teammate Michael Schumacher. The paddock was split between those who believed Dennis had shown good sense and others who saw little honour in fixing a race. Dennis, to put it simply, had placed the interests of his team above the interests of Hamilton, which was another ironic twist when accusations by Alonso later in the season were taken into account.

All in all, it had been a strange Monaco Grand Prix for McLaren. They would leave the principality with maximum points but at least one disgruntled driver and an upcoming hearing with the authorities that could lead to penalties. As this increasingly interesting season unfolded, this was not the last time that McLaren would find themselves in trouble.

RACE RESULT

	DRIVER	TEAM	POINTS
1	Fernando Alonso	McLaren-Mercedes	10
2	Lewis Hamilton	McLaren-Mercedes	8
3	Felipe Massa	Ferrari	6
4	Giancarlo Fisichella	Renault	5
5	Robert Kubica	BMW Sauber	4
6	Nick Heidfeld	BMW Sauber	3
7	Alex Wurz	Williams	2
8	Kimi Räikkönen	Ferrari	1

CONSTRUCTORS' CHAMPIONSHIP AFTER FIVE RACES

	TEAM	POINTS
1	McLaren-Mercedes	76
2	Ferrari	56
3	BMW Sauber	30
4	Renault	16
5	Williams	7
6	Toyota	5
7	Red Bull	4
8	Super Aguri	1

DRIVERS' CHAMPIONSHIP AFTER FIVE RACES

	DRIVER	POINTS
1	Lewis Hamilton	38
1	Fernando Alonso	38
3	Felipe Massa	33
4	Kimi Räikkönen	23
5	Nick Heidfeld	18
6	Giancarlo Fisichella	13
7	Robert Kubica	12
8	Nico Rosberg	5
9	David Coulthard	4
9	Jarno Trulli	4
11	Heikki Kovalainen	3
12	Alex Wurz	2
13	Takuma Sato	1
13	Ralf Schumacher	1

FACING PAGE: Me and my bro – Hamilton with half-brother Nicholas, his biggest fan, at Monaco.

Race 6

Canadian Grand Prix

Montreal

Sunday, 10 June 2007

Attendance: 105,000
Weather: sunny, 27 °C
Track temperature: 50 °C
Number of laps: 70
Circuit length: 2.71 miles
Race distance: 189.7 miles
Fastest lap: Fernando Alonso, 1:16.367 (lap 46)

Hamilton 1st, 10 points (48)

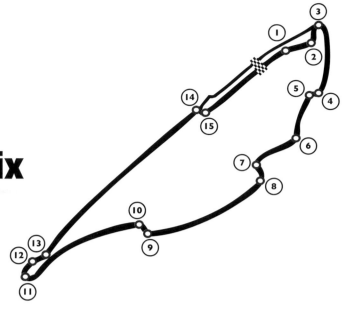

CIRCUIT GILLES VILLENEUVE

The drivers left Monaco and started to focus their attentions on Canada, but what happened on the Côte d'Azure refused to leave McLaren, at least for the following week. It soon became clear that the FIA were anything but amused by the team's decision to prevent Hamilton from launching a full-scale attack on Alonso's race leadership.

The rules were very clear. After the Ferrari fiasco six years earlier, in which they were fined $1 million – half of which was suspended for two years – for a 'breach of podium protocol' – but in reality for Barrichello being told to move over for Schumacher – the Formula One Commission reacted by producing an edict which still applies. The key sentence read, 'Team orders which interfere with a result will be prohibited.'

A day after the Monaco Grand Prix, the sport's governing body issued a statement. 'The FIA have launched an investigation into incidents involving the McLaren-Mercedes team at the Monaco Grand Prix in light of a possible breach of the International Sporting Code,' it said. 'The relevant evidence is under review, and a further announcement will be made in due course.'

As things stood, it was looking likely that McLaren would have to go before the World Motor Sport Council, to be convened in Paris, some time before the Canadian Grand Prix a fortnight after Monaco. Ron Dennis was no fool, however. His words after the race in the principality had been carefully chosen. 'Team strategy is what you bring to win,' he uttered. 'Team orders are what you bring to manipulate a Grand Prix.'

It was with this stance that McLaren responded to the FIA's statement. 'We are completely comfortable with the FIA's investigation with our race strategy and that all the decisions taken both before and during the race were in compliance with the International Sporting Code,' said a spokesman.

The talk in the world of Formula One after this was that Hamilton, far from being compliant with the team orders, not only vented his spleen on the matter down the car radio, but reacted by producing a number of super-quick laps before relenting.

Bernie Ecclestone was far from happy with the situation, either, and let his feelings be known in no small fashion. As far as he was concerned, if McLaren were found to have 'fixed' the race, then the sport

ABOVE: Hamilton practises on the Circuit Gilles Villeneuve during a weekend in Montreal that he will never forget.

should throw the book at them. 'I don't know what the team orders were or are,' Ecclestone said. 'One thing is for sure, though: if there were team orders which related to the position of the two drivers – if somebody was told to move over or hold their position – it is against all sporting regulations we have. If there were orders, then they would be getting off lightly if they get the same sort of fine as Ferrari. They could be excluded from the championship or they could have points deducted. A fine for McLaren, with its money, would not have the same effect as docking points.'

Ecclestone's beef seemed to be with the team, rather than with the drivers. 'If there were instructions, it wouldn't be the drivers' fault. If I'm driving for you and you tell me to stay where I am and not overtake the guy in front, what can I do? It would be those who give the orders who should receive the punishment.'

Former British world champions could not agree on the issue. 'There is an implicit contract between Formula One and the millions who want to watch a

race,' said 1996 world champion Damon Hill. 'That contract is broken when the contestants are asked not to compete against each other.' Nigel Mansell, on the other hand, understood precisely why McLaren took the decision they did. 'Their strategy was perfect,' said the 1992 world champion. 'Alonso was running at a pace necessary to win and there was no point racing to the end as they had beaten all of the opposition. Any team in that circumstance would have made the same call.'

In the end, the FIA agreed with Mansell's point of view and they cleared McLaren of any wrongdoing, ruling that the team had acted within the regulations. 'Having studied the radio traffic between McLaren-Mercedes and its drivers, together with the FIA observer's report and data from the team, it is clear that McLaren's actions were entirely legitimate and no further action is necessary,' read a FIA statement.

Ron Dennis, just a couple of days away from his 60th birthday, was delighted with the outcome. 'The entire team was understandably disappointed that outstanding drives from both Fernando and Lewis, resulting in a great one–two victory and McLaren's 150th win, were temporarily tarnished,' he said. 'The inquiry has removed any doubt about the manner in which the team ran its cars during the 2007 Monaco Grand Prix.'

And so, finally, the world of Formula One could turn its attention to race number six in the calendar in Montreal and a Grand Prix that would make a great deal of news, but this time for all the right reasons. Whatever else Lewis Hamilton goes on to achieve in the sport of Formula One – and it looks likely that it will be a great deal – he will remember the 2007 Canadian Grand Prix for ever. He produced just about the perfect weekend of racing, both for himself and for his team.

To begin with, in Saturday qualifying he secured his first pole position in just his sixth race. Another week, another record for the British star. All season he had threatened to take pole, and it needed a spectacular flying lap at the death to finally succeed, snatching the lead away from teammate Fernando Alonso in the process with a time some four-tenths quicker than the Spaniard's.

The contrast in Hamilton's mood following the post-race press conference in Monaco two weeks earlier could not have been more marked. 'It is a fantastic day for me,' he said afterwards. 'I had to pull it out all the time on that last lap, and it was never easy with the two-time world champion hunting you down. It took a while to get to know the circuit, because it is difficult physically, mentally and technically. It was sweet. We have the car, the team and the strategy, and I know it is going to be tough in the race, but I was really chuffed when they told me I was on P1.

'I had done about five laps on the simulator back at McLaren, but when I went out on Friday I was learning new things all the time. Right now, I want to enjoy the moment. I will go home and have a quiet evening with my dad and my trainer. I am really looking forward to tomorrow, and while Fernando

OVERLEAF: History is made – Hamilton wins his first Formula One Grand Prix, in Canada, at only his sixth attempt.

BELOW: Another drama-filled turn one – Hamilton stays on track in Canada, while teammate Alonso hits the grass.

and I are not going to do anything stupid I want to stay in front.'

Alonso had some team advice to his colleague concerning the next day's race. 'Don't be too aggressive at the first corner and let me through,' he suggested, with a smile. 'I am looking forward to the race. I want to win, but I am not going to win the championship this weekend, so I will be sensible.'

Canada also proved to be a triumphant weekend for BMW Sauber's Nick Heidfeld, beginning with qualification, when he nudged himself into third on the grid, ahead of both Ferraris in fourth and fifth.

Hamilton's successful qualification merely served to create yet more column inches. It seemed that the young man was becoming more and more famous, almost by the day. He appeared to be handling it extremely well, considering how new he was to it all, but on the eve of the Canadian Grand Prix he spoke candidly about his rapidly changing life. 'I don't want people to think I'm an arse,' he admitted. 'At the moment, I believe I'm dealing with it quite well. I hope to stay focused on each weekend's racing. I don't know whether I was born to fame. I know I was born to race and to win. The fame side of it isn't something I particularly enjoy, although some parts of it are cool, and you just have to try and enjoy it.

'It would be nice to do all the racing and win and then disappear to a normal life. I am only five races into the season, and it is gradually getting worse and worse. I am going to be around for a long time, so at some point it will get really bad, and I'll just have to learn to deal with it. I accept being public property, and I'll just have to handle it.'

Besides, it wasn't all bad. The previous week, for example, he met the singer Beyoncé Knowles. 'Things like that wouldn't happen if I wasn't a racing driver,' he reasoned. 'I wouldn't have had the chance to meet her and other great people. I have also had the opportunity to build good relationships with legendary racing figures, such as Sir Jackie Stewart and Sir Stirling Moss. All of this happens because of what I do. It's cool meeting Sir Jackie, but it was really wicked talking to Beyoncé. She is serious, incredible and beautiful. She invited me to her concert at Wembley. I sat in the crowd, and people started to notice me. It was getting a bit wild. Fortunately, I had my cousin's boyfriend with me. He's a big Nigerian guy, so he stood up and made out to be a bouncer.'

The anger over McLaren's team tactics in Monaco had also subsided. 'There's a saying that goes, "Never bite the hand that feeds you,"' Hamilton explained. 'Ron and I have respect for each other, and I am racing for his team. If it were not for him, I wouldn't have been racing these past few years. If I do a good job, then I pay him back with success.'

A huge slab of payment was made the very next day at the Gilles Villeneuve circuit. Lewis Hamilton, in just his sixth Formula One Grand Prix, led the race from start to finish, except briefly after he had made his first pit stop, taking the chequered flag over four seconds ahead of Nick Heidfeld, with Williams's Alex Wurz grabbing a surprising third place. Other unheralded drivers also made the most of a dramatic Grand Prix in which so many experienced campaigners lost their heads on an unforgiving circuit. Renault's Heikki Kovalainen recorded a fourth as he began to justify the promise everyone felt the young Finn had. Räikkönen could only trail in fifth, but at least that was better than Alonso, who only managed seventh, one ahead of Ralf Schumacher, who grabbed an unexpected point in his Toyota, but one behind Takuma Sato in his Super Aguri. With all due respect to Sato, that just about summed up Alonso's day.

To say the Spaniard had a race he would like to forget would be an understatement. The world champion went off on four different occasions on turn one, suffered a time penalty for sinning under the safety car, was overtaken by Sato and was black-flagged for leaving the pit lane under a red light.

The drama began to unfold as early as turn one. Hamilton made a textbook start from pole, first moving over to block Alonso, then returning to his racing line to take the first corner in the lead. Alonso was so desperate to grab first place that he missed the turn completely, allowing Heidfeld to cruise into second place. It was a desperate start for the double world champion, embarrassed by the rookie and now stuck behind the BMW Sauber on a lighter fuel load.

Hamilton took full advantage in ruthless fashion. As each lap flashed past, he increased his lead over the slower Heidfeld, with Alonso stuck behind. By lap nineteen, as Alonso went off at turn one for the third out of four times, allowing Massa to overtake him and relegate him to fourth place, Hamilton was out of sight.

While he cruised to a straightforward victory, driving as if it was his sixtieth Grand Prix not his sixth, mayhem was taking place behind him. On lap 22, the safety car was deployed after Adrian Sutil's Spyker crashed. During the next lap, Alonso and Nico Rosberg incurred stop–go penalties. On lap 27, Robert Kubica's spectacular accident meant another visit from the safety car, and it reappeared for a third time on lap 50 after Christijan Albers also crashed in his Spyker. Six laps later, it came out for a staggering fourth time when Vitantonio Liuzzi crashed.

The end result was Lewis Hamilton's first-ever win in Formula One, and by virtue of scoring ten points to Alonso's paltry two he had suddenly leapt into a healthy eight-point lead in the drivers' championship. He also became the nineteenth British racing driver in history to win a FIA World Championship Grand Prix, notching up an amazing one hundred and ninety-second victory for Britain, placing them way above second-placed Germany in the table, who had managed 103 wins in comparison.

Afterwards, the rookie who seemed to have the world at his feet was understandably emotional. 'It has been a fantastic day,' he said. 'This is history. To come here for the first time and win is unbelievable. For me, it's been an incredible season already. I've been ready to win for some time now. I've had a feeling that it was just a matter of when and where. It's really hard to grasp everything. I feel like I'm on a different planet right now. Going into this weekend, I really did sense it was going to be my time. To get pole and win was a dream. It's taken me to another level.'

It certainly had. Damon Hill was impressed enough to make an admission. 'I've never seen a rookie like him,' he said. 'I don't think anybody has.'

Martin Whitmarsh, McLaren's chief executive, was also moved to add his own praise. 'It's pretty clear that Lewis ticks all the necessary boxes,' he said. 'If the trend continues, there is no reason why he could not become the greatest driver ever.' And that was coming from a man who had worked with Senna, Prost and Mika Häkkinen.

BELOW: That's my boy! Anthony and Lewis Hamilton hug after the rookie beats the world to win in Canada.

Murray Walker, who had seen a great champion or two in his time, was also astounded by what he had just witnessed. Now 83, but with his wits as sharp as ever, Walker said, 'I've been watching Formula One since it began in 1950, and I've never seen anything like this in my life. There just aren't enough superlatives for what Lewis is doing race after race. It was quite incredible when he finished on the podium in his first Grand Prix, and now he's been on the podium for six successive races – four second places, a third place and now a victory. It is unprecedented in the history of Formula One. It is more than feasible that he could win the world championship this year.'

Another delighted onlooker was team boss Ron Dennis, who saw another healthy return on the investment he'd made on Hamilton all those years before. 'It was a textbook drive from Lewis,' was his reaction to another McLaren victory. 'He didn't put a foot wrong. His drive was faultless, and he did not have one single thing gifted to him. It was a race he won. That makes it a special win, because the first win for many drivers, which is sometimes their only win, comes from circumstances that are unusual to the event. This was a straight-out, full-on, tremendous achievement and at one of the most difficult circuits in the world, and he deserves all the plaudits he will undoubtedly get.'

The first person Hamilton sought after jumping victoriously from his car was Anthony, who had taken every step of the journey with his son. 'I have to dedicate this victory to my dad,' an emotional Hamilton added. 'Without him it would not have been possible. I could see him from the podium. He obviously had a tear in his eye. And I want to say hello to all my family back home, who I know were watching, the fans and the team back in Woking and Stuttgart. At the end, I wanted to do cartwheels. It was extremely emotional driving back to the pits. The fans were unbelievable.'

Anthony Hamilton, still wiping away tears long after the presentation of prizes and playing of national anthems, was very conscious of the potential pitfalls of such extraordinary and sudden success. 'If you start to become someone you are not, then you will fall flat on your face,' he explained. 'It's just about remaining normal. But I am just so proud of Lewis. This has been his and our dream for so long, and now he's realised it.'

His son's review of how he had won his first-ever Formula One Grand Prix was as clinical as the manner of victory. 'It wasn't the best start for me, especially with Fernando flying past me at the first corner,' he admitted. 'I'm not sure what happened. Then Fernando went wide. I didn't want that, obviously. He went straight, and I got a fantastic exit. After that, it was a fairly smooth race for me. The team did a great job calling me in before the first safety car. Three times I had to build a lead. Each time, the tyres and brakes got cold. It is so easy to put it into the wall in those situations. But I held it together until the end.'

Carnage had been at work all around him: Alonso had a torrid afternoon, only finishing seventh; Kubica's crash was the biggest of the season and yet, amazingly, he emerged with nothing more than a sprained ankle and concussion; and Anthony Davidson ran over an unfortunate groundhog that emerged from the riverside, forcing the British Super Aguri driver to lock up his brakes and make an unscheduled pit stop for a new front wing.

All eyes now turned to the second Grand Prix on Formula One's North American leg. Could Hamilton win again? He could not see a reason why not. 'If I produce the same drive and keep the same focus, then there's every chance I can back this win up in Montreal with another at Indianapolis,' he reasoned.

The win, and Alonso's disappointing result, had propelled the rookie to a significant lead in the race for the drivers' title. What with that and even greater confidence stemming from his achievement in Canada, the rest of the Formula One grid now realised they had a serious problem on their hands. The double world champion knew for sure that he would have to fight very hard simply to be the best driver in his team, never mind the world.

FACING PAGE: Tastes good! How much better does champagne taste when you have just won a Grand Prix for the first time?

RACE RESULT			
	DRIVER	TEAM	POINTS
1	Lewis Hamilton	McLaren-Mercedes	10
2	Nick Heidfeld	BMW Sauber	8
3	Alex Wurz	Williams	6
4	Heikki Kovalainen	Renault	5
5	Kimi Räikkönen	Ferrari	4
6	Takuma Sato	Super Aguri	3
7	Fernando Alonso	McLaren-Mercedes	2
8	Ralf Schumacher	Toyota	1

DRIVERS' CHAMPIONSHIP AFTER SIX RACES		
	DRIVER	POINTS
1	Lewis Hamilton	48
2	Fernando Alonso	40
3	Felipe Massa	33
4	Kimi Räikkönen	27
5	Nick Heidfeld	26
6	Giancarlo Fisichella	13
7	Robert Kubica	12
8	Alex Wurz	8
8	Heikki Kovalainen	8
10	Nico Rosberg	5
11	David Coulthard	4
11	Takuma Sato	4
11	Jarno Trulli	4
14	Ralf Schumacher	2

CONSTRUCTORS' CHAMPIONSHIP AFTER SIX RACES		
	TEAM	POINTS
1	McLaren-Mercedes	88
2	Ferrari	60
3	BMW Sauber	38
4	Renault	21
5	Williams	13
6	Toyota	6
7	Red Bull	4
7	Super Aguri	4

Race 7

US Grand Prix

Indianapolis

Sunday, 17 June 2007

Attendance: not released but approximately 120,000
Weather: humid, 35 °C
Track temperature: 45 °C
Number of laps: 73
Circuit length: 2.605 miles
Race distance: 190.165 miles
Fastest lap: Kimi Räikkönen, 1:13.117 (lap 49)

INDIANAPOLIS MOTOR SPEEDWAY

Hamilton 1st, 10 points (58)

As the Formula One circus made the relatively short journey across the Canadian–American border and down to Indianapolis, leading figures from other teams had seen enough of Hamilton, the new phenomenon, to praise him. One such figure was Sir Frank Williams, the legendary boss of the Williams Formula One team that has won so many Grands Prix and employed so many world champions, despite experiencing a leaner spell in the past decade. 'We have never seen anything like this in Formula One before,' said the man who was in charge of Ayrton Senna for many years. 'It's almost inexplicable. I think the word phenomenon just about fits. It makes you think that maybe there is a God after all. He is a great story, and not just for Ron Dennis and McLaren, but for everybody involved in motor sport.'

The paddock seemed unanimous on this verdict, but a new belief had also invaded the sport: that Hamilton's teammate, double world champion Fernando Alonso, was starting to become rattled by what was going on. After all, he was supposed to be the star at McLaren, not the kid from Tewin. Mike Gascoyne, who assisted Alonso to his first world

title as chief designer at Renault, had identified the first signs of a problem between the two McLaren drivers. 'You have to say that Lewis is the favourite for the world championship,' he argued. 'Fernando looked ragged. How many times did he go off at turn one? Lewis just cruised it. The most impressive thing for me was how Lewis made it look so simple. It is the most impressive thing I've seen in many, many years. Who's going to stop him? The best make it look easy. That's clearly what Lewis is going to be. If Fernando had done that, we would have said it was a masterclass. But the young lad did it. Now he's going to Indianapolis believing he can win there, too, and why not? McLaren look absolutely dominant.'

Niki Lauda, who had already liked what he had seen earlier in the season, was another motor-racing icon happy to eulogise on the rookie's behalf. 'So you Brits have a new guy,' he said. 'He is the best rookie ever, and his future is very bright, because he still has so much time to improve as a driver. To win in only his sixth race is incredible. He blew Alonso off in the same car, which is always the most difficult thing. He is the quickest and the best.'

Listening to this was a bemused Anthony

2007 FORMULA 1™ UNITED STATES GRAND PRIX

Hamilton. He had always believed in his son and had always dreamt of times such as these, but never, not in his wildest dreams, could he have imagined the six-race start Lewis had made to his Formula One career, culminating with a journey to Indianapolis with a Grand Prix win under his belt from the week before. 'I don't know what's coming next,' Anthony admitted. 'I'm practically speechless. Lewis has confounded logic from the start. It's frightening really. I know he's loving it. A lot of young guys in karts dream about being a Formula One driver. We have an opportunity, and we don't want to waste it. People said you don't put rookies in a McLaren, you put them in a Minardi. People don't want to believe, but you have to believe in the youngsters. We never made plans to get where we are. We just wanted to be the best we could.'

On the Tuesday before the US Grand Prix, the first real evidence of a rift in the McLaren camp became clear after Alonso publicly claimed on Spanish radio that his teammate had been 'very lucky' to win in Canada, as well as complaining that he believed McLaren favoured Hamilton. The 'lucky' tag came about because of the events during the race. The safety car had been deployed just after Hamilton had

ABOVE: Pole position – Hamilton answers questions at the post-qualifying press conference, having grabbed pole in Indianapolis, while a disgruntled, second-placed Alonso looks on.

FACING PAGE: Mentor and prodigy – Ron Dennis gives the man he's supported for 12 years a pep talk at the US Grand Prix.

made it out of the pits following his first fuel stop. Alonso, low on fuel at the time, had been forced to pit while the safety car was lapping in order to avoid grinding to a halt on the track. This was in breach of the rules, and the Spaniard had incurred a ten-second stop–go penalty, which had seen him drop from third to seventh. 'Lewis's win is very good for the team,' Alonso said. 'But it was very lucky as well, as we were on very similar strategies, and if the safety car comes out one lap before Lewis's stop, we would have been eighth and ninth.'

Perhaps the more serious accusation, though, was the one he made concerning favouritism. 'Right from the start, I have never felt totally comfortable,' he told the Spanish radio station. 'I have a British teammate in a British team. He's doing a great job, and we know that all the support and help is going to him. I understood that from the beginning.'

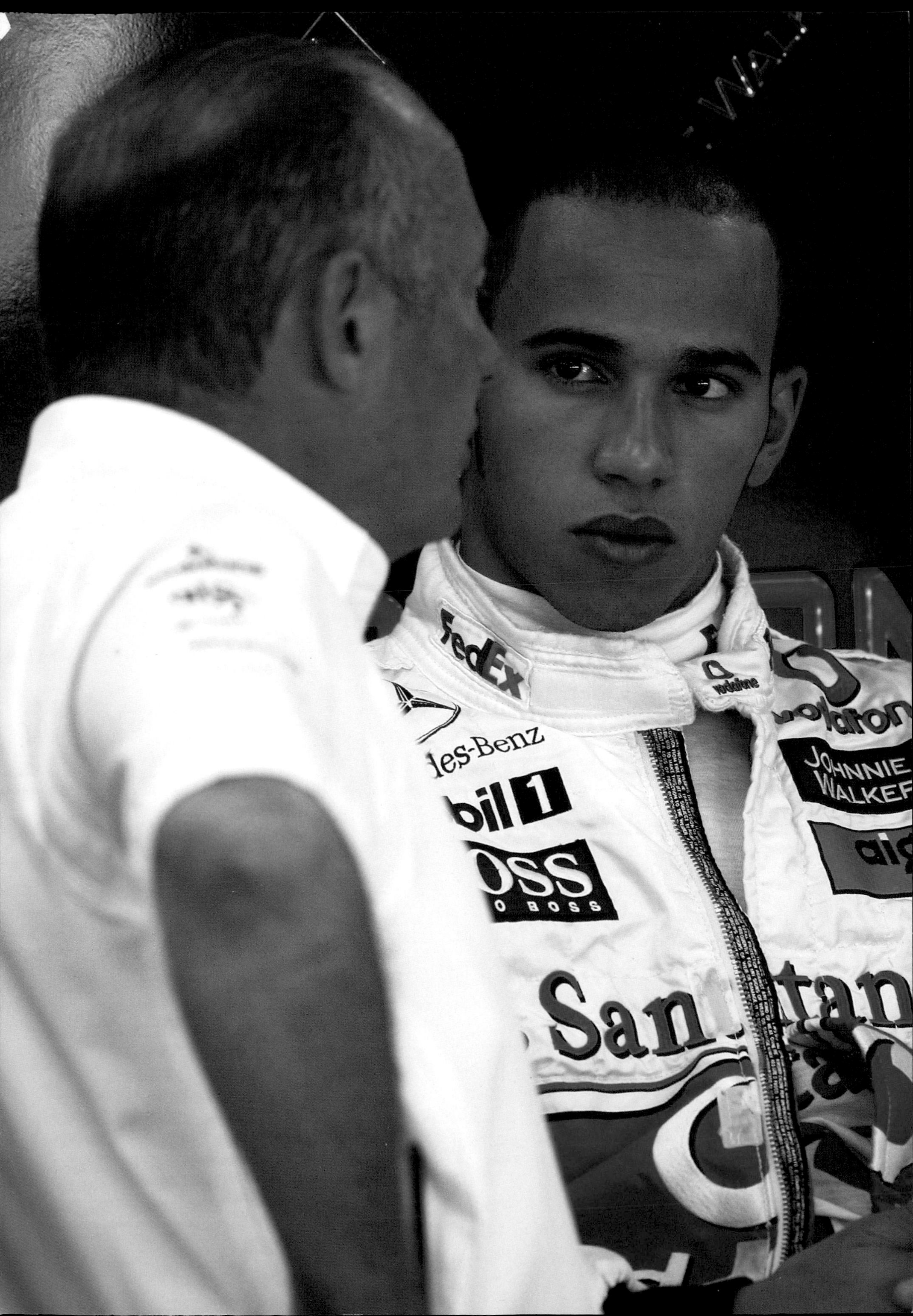
FedEx
JOHNNIE
WALKER

It forced Ron Dennis to insist that all drivers were equal at McLaren. 'There is a healthy competition between the teams working on each car – this is inevitable and there is no issue with that,' he said. 'However, I can categorically state once again that both drivers have equal equipment and equal support. Fernando and Lewis know this and support this. Fernando hasn't been with the team long, and the relationship can only continue to develop.'

At that point in the season, Alonso was not too concerned. He knew there were still 11 races to go. The eventual title would be decided further down the line. 'I've won two races out of six, and I've finished on the podium four times,' he argued. 'I'm calm, I'm fine, but I know there's an impatience to return to the top and dominate. I'm second in the championship. I'm eight points behind. I would be worse off if I were at Renault or Honda or any other team. At the moment, I am where I expected to be and with a clear chance of winning the title in Brazil in October. Not now after six races.'

The attempt at sounding relaxed was a little too late. His comments to Spanish listeners caused uproar, and when the drivers arrived at The Brickyard – the fans' name for Indianapolis – this seemed to be the only topic of discussion. But Alonso was not prepared to back down from his earlier view. 'I said I was not totally comfortable, and that's because there are things missing,' he explained. 'I've talked to the team about it, and things must be done in the way I think they should be done. Obviously, it's something between the team and me. That's the way I think, and there's nothing more to it. It starts and ends there.'

Confusingly, he said all this and yet still insisted he was relaxed. 'I'm happy with everything,' said the 25 year old. 'My life is fantastic and with the team as well. I know that this week has been quite difficult after my comments in Spain. I think these comments are quite normal. There are no complaints.'

As usual, the paddock was left to work out the riddles. In short, Alonso was making it clear that as double world champion he expected primary treatment at McLaren and a greater input into the team. Dennis had always operated a no-favouritism policy. Alonso and his advisers, not comfortable with this, suspected Hamilton was favoured in any case. Alonso's radio comments were his way of making his discomfort known.

The other drivers were watching developments

with interest, none more so than Jenson Button, who had experienced some of the mania Hamilton was now living through. Before Hamilton arrived on the scene, Button was the darling of the British motor-racing public and media, but a combination of the rookie's startling impact and his own Honda team's failure to produce a competitive car left him looking wistfully on. 'In a Renault, I don't think any driver would beat Fernando,' he argued. 'With McLaren, I'm sure it's a very different car and different feeling. If you look at his style in a Renault last year, it was very different from anyone else's on the grid, and it worked for him. Maybe Lewis is doing a better job than he expected, but Fernando is still an exceptional driver and one of the best in the world, as he has shown in the last couple of years. It's just not working for him at the moment.'

The Spaniard could clutch at the fact that Hamilton had never raced any kind of car at Indianapolis before.

His experience of The Brickyard came down to video footage, studying technological data and playing on his PlayStation. 'Watching the Indy 500 over the years, it's an awesome race and I've always wanted to go and watch as a spectator,' the 22 year old said. 'But to be racing here is pretty cool. Just flying over, I could see what the track was like. It's a great complex, and I'm gunning for victory.'

At Friday's first practice, he finished third quickest, some seven-tenths behind Alonso, but come Saturday's official qualifying and it was, not for the first time that season, a different story. Hamilton, for the second time in eight days, claimed pole position – his second career pole – while Alonso had to make do with accompanying his teammate on the front row of the grid. Once again, the Ferraris of Massa and Räikkönen made up the second row, in third and fourth respectively, and, once again, the BMW Sauber of Nick Heidfeld came in fifth fastest. With Kubica

ABOVE: Waiting to pounce – Alonso is on his teammate's tail, but Hamilton holds off the double world champion at Indianapolis.

sitting this race out after his big crash in Montreal, Sebastian Vettel, the next German wunderkind, was given a chance to drive and impressed with a seventh place in qualifying behind the rapidly improving Finn Heikki Kovalainen, who was beginning to overshadow Giancarlo Fisichella, his more illustrious teammate at Renault.

Hamilton was understandably delighted with his second successive pole and seemed to be enjoying the moment at his McLaren teammate's expense. 'I knew Fernando would go for it on his last lap, and I'm surprised he didn't go quicker,' he said afterwards, after he finished less than 0.2 seconds ahead of his rival. 'I really thought he'd get pole here. He has been quicker all weekend. My last two laps were spot on, though. Perfect! Getting my second pole was even better than

ABOVE: Hamilton fans show their support for the driver and their country in Indianapolis.

last week, and it's great to see so many British flags. I couldn't be happier. In fact, I'm ecstatic.'

If he felt that way on the Saturday evening, just imagine his emotions one day later after he had secured his second win in Formula One, a second successive victory and another ten points, increasing his lead in the world drivers' championship to ten. However, it was not just the fact that he had won again, beating Alonso into second place, that was so satisfying; it was the manner in which he had pulled it off.

Formula One has sometimes struggled to make an impact in the United States, where Nascar and IRL (Indy Racing League) rule. It did not help matters when the US Grand Prix was won by Michael Schumacher's Ferrari against barely any meaningful opposition in 2005, following a change in the track layout and a refusal by some teams to compete. But the 2007 race had it all, from the very first corner to the very last. It was an old-fashioned shoot-out in the American Midwest. The tension was there even before the start, thanks to Alonso's midweek utterances. A team meeting on the eve of the race was said to have cleared the air, but come Sunday afternoon on the track the gloves were quite clearly off.

Another sign of the changing times was provided by American rapper Pharrell Williams, who had just become a Lewis Hamilton fan. The global star had been given a guided tour of the McLaren garage by Anthony Hamilton in the morning, and when Hamilton junior held off Alonso to round the first turn in first place Williams was clearly seen pumping his fists with delight. Alonso did manage to draw level with his young rival as they careered down to the first corner but wisely decided to hold off when it became

pole was one thing; having a double world champion stalking you just half a second behind, producing overtaking moves at almost every corner and each time they hurtled down the long straight at Indianapolis at speeds of over 200 mph, was another.

It was at the start of the 39th lap when the drama reached its zenith. The world champion drew his car alongside Hamilton as both flashed down the start–finish straight. Back on the pit wall, Ron Dennis and his McLaren colleagues must have feared the worst. Either Alonso was going to overtake the young upstart or there was going to be a horrendous crash.

In the event, neither happened. Alonso moved, Hamilton hit back, their tyres all but touched and the younger man somehow held on. The Spaniard would continue his all-out assault on his teammate, at least up to the 50th lap when he went to the pits, and when Hamilton emerged from the pit lane a lap later he found himself 50 metres in front of the world champion. However, it was the duel on the straight that was the defining moment of the race and one of the defining moments of the season. Others may have folded under the considerable pressure Alonso was exerting; Hamilton simply refused to buckle.

Alonso continued to dog his man for the next 20 laps and right up to the very end, when he finished just 1.5 seconds behind his teammate, but he discovered a new and disconcerting fact that day. Not only was Hamilton quick, he also possessed big balls. Now, more than ever, Alonso realised he would have to fight like never before to become world champion.

Behind them, the Ferraris had their own private battle, with Räikkönen edging to within 0.4 seconds of Massa at one point, but the Brazilian held on to third place and the Finn had to make do with fourth. Kovalainen's rise continued with a fifth place, Trulli was sixth, Mark Webber scored his first points of the season in his Red Bull in seventh and young Vettel impressed in his first race in eighth. In doing so, he became the youngest Formula One points scorer ever at nineteen years, eleven months and fourteen days, beating Jenson Button's twenty years, two months and seven days. Nico Rosberg could count himself unlucky, as he was forced to retire his Williams after the engine blew whilst in sixth place with just four laps remaining.

Hamilton, of course, notched up more firsts in this incredible debut year. His second win made it seven successive podiums in his first seven races, and he also became the first rookie ever to win a US Grand Prix

clear that there was no way through. The race would be long, and he would have plenty of opportunities to show who was boss. Or so he thought.

Further down the grid, David Coulthard, Rubens Barrichello and Ralf Schumacher all tangled on the first lap and were out of the race, while Räikkönen's poor start saw him slip from fourth to sixth. However, the pulses really began to race from the 21st lap. This was when Hamilton made his first stop, together with Massa and Heidfeld. Alonso followed suit one lap later and was all over the rookie from that moment onwards as the two McLarens provided the most entertaining racing yet seen that remarkable season. When the Spaniard rejoined from the pit lane, he was behind both Hamilton and Jarno Trulli. He soon put paid to the Italian, and by the 32nd lap he had reduced Hamilton's lead to a mere 0.6 seconds. This was the ultimate test for the young British driver. Leading from at Indianapolis. Emerson Fittipaldi also secured a US Grand Prix win in his rookie year in 1970, but the race was staged at Watkins Glen.

Afterwards, there was more joy from the man who now knew that he would be leading the world championship at his home race, the British Grand Prix at Silverstone, regardless of events at the next race on the calendar, the French Grand Prix. 'What a dream,' said Hamilton. 'This is a great leap in my career and in my life. Thanks to my family, God and to the team. I never thought in a million years I'd be here with these drivers and win at both these tracks I didn't know. I've fully enjoyed it. These have been the best two races of my life.'

Reflecting on the tough duel with Alonso, Hamilton said, 'It was pressure all the way, especially in the second stint. Fernando was up my tail. He fought very well and professionally. I pulled a gap at the end, but it was a long, hard day. I got a lot of energy from the supporters. The laps went on and on. They said on the radio that there were 15 laps to go. It seemed a lifetime, especially being in the lead. I was able to do it, and I'm very, very emotional. It's a perfect team, and this is the icing on the cake.'

Only the previous month, the Scottish driver Dario Franchitti had also won at The Brickyard, finishing the world-famous Indy 500 in front. He would go on to secure the IRL drivers' title, which made it a magnificent year for British motor racing. Now another British driver had also won at the Indianapolis Motor Speedway.

'It's brilliant to win any race, but to win here is special,' Hamilton continued. 'I've grown up watching the Indy 500. It was great for the country when Dario won last month. I'm thrilled to follow suit. Coming into the season, you have to be realistic. I had an open mind

and hoped to do well. I hoped I might get a podium at some point. I've been on the podium every race. It's just insane. I find it very hard to come to terms with everything. I don't think anybody expected it.'

Certainly not Fernando Alonso. If he was seething inside, he somehow managed to keep it hidden from the rest of the world. 'We knew from the winter tests that Lewis was quick,' he said after again finishing second best to his teammate. 'So why not fight for podiums, victories and championships? On the other hand, it has been a surprise for me and everybody else to see him doing so well and leading the championship at this point. It was very close in the race, but I couldn't manage to overtake. I tried in the middle stint. We got side by side at the end of the straight but not enough to overtake him. The start of the race was the key. I lost position in Canada. You don't want to finish the race in first corner. Eight points are better than nothing.'

Now everyone was talking about the very real possibility of Lewis Hamilton, a rookie, becoming world champion. The man himself was wise not to get too carried away with the prospect. 'It's too early for that,' he said. 'Seven races into the championship, I have to be smart and realise that I'm running at the front. There is a chance of winning the championship, but I'm not getting my hopes up. I'm just trying to stay consistent and focused.'

This response was fair enough, but the facts spoke for themselves. Seven races, seven podiums, including two wins, fifty-eight points and an average of 8.28 points per race. The last time a British driver won both the Canadian and US Grands Prix in a McLaren was 1976. That man was James Hunt, and he went on to become world champion. Twenty-one years on and the omens were looking increasingly good for Lewis Hamilton.

FACING PAGE: The boy's a winner! At Indianapolis, Hamilton notches up a second successive victory to follow his triumph in Canada.

RACE RESULT

	DRIVER	TEAM	POINTS
1	Lewis Hamilton	McLaren-Mercedes	10
2	Fernando Alonso	McLaren-Mercedes	8
3	Felipe Massa	Ferrari	6
4	Kimi Räikkönen	Ferrari	5
5	Heikki Kovalainen	Renault	4
6	Jarno Trulli	Toyota	3
7	Mark Webber	Red Bull	2
8	Sebastian Vettel	BMW Sauber	1

CONSTRUCTORS' CHAMPIONSHIP AFTER SEVEN RACES

	TEAM	POINTS
1	McLaren-Mercedes	106
2	Ferrari	71
3	BMW Sauber	39
4	Renault	25
5	Williams	13
6	Toyota	9
7	Red Bull	6
8	Super Aguri	4

DRIVERS' CHAMPIONSHIP AFTER SEVEN RACES

	DRIVER	POINTS
1	Lewis Hamilton	58
2	Fernando Alonso	48
3	Felipe Massa	39
4	Kimi Räikkönen	32
5	Nick Heidfeld	26
6	Giancarlo Fisichella	13
7	Robert Kubica	12
7	Heikki Kovalainen	12
9	Alex Wurz	8
10	Jarno Trulli	7
11	Nico Rosberg	5
12	David Coulthard	4
12	Takuma Sato	4
14	Mark Webber	2
14	Ralf Schumacher	2
16	Sebastian Vettel	1

Race 8

French Grand Prix

Magny-Cours

Sunday, 1 July 2007

Attendance: 72,000
Weather: humid, 25 °C
Track temperature: 40 °C
Number of laps: 70
Circuit length: 2.741 miles
Race distance: 191.87 miles
Fastest lap: Felipe Massa, 1:16.099 (lap 42)

Hamilton 3rd, 6 points (64)

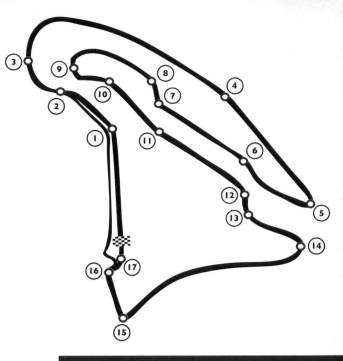

CIRCUIT DE NEVERS MAGNY-COURS

When Lewis Hamilton left European shores, he was already the most talked-about driver on the Formula One grid. When he returned, after his two-race sojourn in North America, he was a winner and a man now favoured to be world champion. The fact that he was a rookie made this all the more incredible. 'Lewismania' had really hit the streets of Britain, and McLaren, although delighted at the success of a young man they had nurtured for so many years, had a phenomenon on their hands – and someone who was suddenly in phenomenal demand. Add to this the signs of the team's two drivers being at odds with one other, and McLaren boss Ron Dennis had quite a problem on his hands, one that he had never really experienced before.

'It's a new experience for all of us,' Dennis conceded as McLaren and the other teams pitched up at Silverstone for three days of testing before the two back-to-back Grands Prix in France and then the UK. 'I'm just trying to use common sense to make sure we handle everything the right way.

'We've all had a bit of a skirmish in the early races. We have seen both drivers caught up in things. They have to be monstrously careful about how they talk about each other to the press. We want to be thinking what a great achievement this is, rather than waiting to put the next fire out. It is clearly an unusual set of circumstances. What we have now is even more exciting than anything Michael Schumacher gave us, and he gave us a lot.'

If anyone doubted McLaren's policy of allowing both drivers equal chances to race, then Indianapolis would have quelled any lingering doubts. 'I was holding my breath,' Dennis admitted, referring to the absorbing moment when his two drivers drew level at 200 mph down the start–finish straight. 'It was a hero-to-zero moment. Nothing demonstrates more than that just how much our drivers are allowed to race. It's going to be a great season for us. They will have every opportunity to compete. It's stressful but manageable. Alonso is behind but in the fortunate position of being in a car that can win.'

As for Hamilton, his mentor realised life would never quite be the same again for him. 'His life will obviously change. There is an inevitability about that. The invasion of his privacy will become a big issue. He will have to find somewhere to live to avoid that. I don't know whether he'll be able to continue to do

ABOVE: The pit lane at the French Grand Prix, with Hamilton's section of the McLaren-Mercedes garage in the centre.

ABOVE: Great mates – Hamilton and Spyker's Adrian Sutil swap stories during practice for the French Grand Prix.

FACING PAGE: What's wrong with the car? Hamilton looks on after breaking down during practice at Magny-Cours.

things as he did before. We have spoken about this with him. The important thing is to ensure it does not impact negatively on his racing.'

Anthony Hamilton was confident this would not happen. 'What we do is the work at the track, get wrapped up in that for as long as necessary, and then go to our house and live our lives, where nothing can touch us, when there is no need to be anything other than ourselves,' he explained. 'However focused you are, however clear your intentions are, there might be a danger of some things changing. Reality might be threatened, but in Lewis's case I just don't think it's a threat. He has always known where he is.'

What, though, if the going got tough, as it surely would at some point in the season and most definitely at some point in his career? Would such a young man who had experienced little else but success be able to deal with things when the chips were down? 'I understand that people might assume Lewis is so new to everything he might be rattled if things suddenly go wrong,' Anthony responded. 'What they don't know about is all the years Lewis has known what it is to lose as much as what it is to win. For 14 years, he has been winning and losing and going into all the grey areas in between. So, no, I don't doubt his ability to deal with setbacks. That said, he has never considered the possibility of anything more than the odd reverse, which comes in any career and any life. Blips? They come to everybody. The key is how you deal with them.'

Another respected figure in motor sport picked up on this point: Dutchman Kees van de Grint, the chief engineer of Bridgestone, the solo tyre suppliers to Formula One after Michelin's withdrawal at the end of the 2006 season. While Alonso had been using Michelin with Renault, Hamilton had been driving on Bridgestones during his winning 2006 season in GP2. 'Can Lewis win the world title this year?' asked van de Grint. 'Why not? He has the fastest car, and he is beating the world champion, who is in the same car, fair and square. We'll have to wait and see if he turns out better than Michael Schumacher. We can judge Michael on a whole career, whereas Lewis is right at the start of his. Michael was so great, because when things weren't going so well he won races that normally would not have been won.

'I'd say you learn most about people when things aren't going well, so we'll have to wait and see with Lewis. Certainly, you would be a fool to bet against him this year. He has shown extreme talent. I do not understand when people say he is too young, too inexperienced, and I really hope what he is doing will be an inspiration for young people across the world. The most impressive thing about Lewis is that I haven't seen him make a mistake yet. He has been so much in charge of himself.'

Another believer was David Coulthard, the oldest

and most experienced man on the grid. The Scot had driven for McLaren for many years, had 13 Grand Prix wins under his belt and had raced against some of the greatest names in the sport, from Senna and Prost to Schumacher, so he knew what he was talking about. 'How good is Lewis?' he asked himself. 'Undoubtedly, the guy is very special. I'd say he is a combination of Senna and Prost. He possesses Senna's natural talent, confidence and aggression, but also Prost's smoothness and patience. That's a pretty impressive cocktail, but Lewis has got it. We had Senna and Prost, Mansell and [Nelson] Piquet, then Michael Schumacher. We have now just entered the Lewis Hamilton era.'

Unlike the general public, who perceived Hamilton's success to have been achieved almost overnight, the drivers already knew all about the youngster, but they were still surprised by the impact the 22 year old had made in his first season at the highest level of motor sport. 'Ask any of the drivers and they'd all say they knew all about Lewis before he joined Formula One, but it's his performances that have

really taken us aback,' explained Coulthard. 'He's a Formula One rookie, and in seven races so far he's produced virtually flawless drives. Supposedly better and more experienced drivers like Fernando and Kimi Räikkönen have been making mistakes, but not Lewis. The fact that he's beaten fair and square his teammate and double world champion is very, very impressive.'

The Red Bull driver also bore witness to the fact that Alonso was rattled. 'There's no doubt about it,' he continued. 'Fernando's all at sea at the moment, and he's showing his Latin temperament. He's had a couple of off-days, unlike Lewis, and that's why he finds himself ten points behind his teammate, but he's not just going to give up, is he? He's going to try everything he can to win a third successive world title, and there's still two-thirds of the season remaining.

'As each race passes, so the pressure will grow on Lewis. Right now, he's still so young, everything is still so new and he's enjoying himself so much that I doubt he's feeling any pressure at all. He's going to have an incredible amount of support at Silverstone,

ABOVE: Räikkönen bites back – brilliant but inconsistent, this is one of his good days as Kimi Räikkönen leads Hamilton on his way to winning the French Grand Prix.

and Ron Dennis at McLaren is just about the best man to ensure he is protected from too many outside interests and that he gets on with the job. But the journey he has started is a long one.'

As for the manner in which he expected the rest of the season to pan out, Coulthard had little doubt. 'McLaren will win the constructors' title, of that there's no doubt, and their drivers will be first and second in the drivers' title race.' In what order, though? 'Based on the evidence of the first seven races, I have to say that it's looking very good for Lewis to become world champion in his first year in Formula One. And that, regardless of how good his car may be, would really be something.'

Hamilton got a sense of his new-found popularity back in his home country when he was given a rousing reception at the Goodwood Festival of Speed. It was nothing compared with what would be waiting for

him at Silverstone, and he was itching to get to the Northamptonshire circuit, but first came Magny-Cours and a track, unlike Montreal and Indianapolis, that he had plenty of experience of – and not all of it good. 'It's not been one of my best circuits to race at,' Hamilton admitted on arriving at the famous old racetrack. 'The French round of the GP2 championship last season was not my best weekend, as I had a coming-together in the first race. That led to me starting from 19th. I did make my way up the field to fifth to score some points, so at least that proves it's possible to overtake here.

'Of course, you want to be on pole here, as you do at every race, but you can pass at Magny-Cours, while there is a short pit lane that means there are more strategy options. It is not as much of a penalty when you stop for tyres and fuel. At the moment, I'm obviously looking forward to the British Grand Prix at Silverstone, because it's my home circuit, but I know I must first score points here in France to maintain my lead in the drivers' championship.'

Alonso, his chief rival, remained positive, leaning on his victory at Monaco, even if it had been in controversial circumstances. 'Although Magny-Cours and Monaco have very different characteristics in general, there are some similarities between them too,' he said. 'They both have a lot of tight, twisty corners, so given how well the car performed at Monaco I am looking forward to getting it out on the track. I'm feeling really motivated right now.'

While everyone was focusing on the battle at McLaren, people seemed to have forgotten that Ferrari possessed two outstanding drivers of their own, neither of whom had been happy with the way the season had shaped up so far. At Magny-Cours, they exploded out of their garages during Friday's free practice to post the quickest times, and during the Saturday official qualifying they were at it again.

Only Hamilton stood in the way of a Ferrari one–two on the front row of the grid. However, after clinching pole in his last two races, he had to make do with second place this time, Massa beating him by seven-hundredths of a second as the Brazilian won their head-to-head on the flying lap. Räikkönen claimed third and Kubica, back in the BMW Sauber hot seat after missing out in Indianapolis following his horrific crash in Montreal, recorded a highly creditable fourth. As for Alonso, his challenge to Hamilton seemed to be going from bad to worse. At Magny-Cours, he could only start in tenth place on the grid after managing

LEFT: Another season for D.C. – David Coulthard was still proving his worth for Red Bull midway through his fourteenth season in Formula One.

just one lap in the third and final part of qualifying before retiring to the pits with a gearbox problem.

That evening, Hamilton was far from disappointed at ending his streak of pole positions. 'I'm the rookie, and this is my first season,' he reminded everybody, as if he had to justify himself. 'A lot of the drivers understand this. In fact, they probably expect me to make a mistake at some point, but I'm here to prove them wrong. You can't be perfect all the time. I thought I had pole, and it would have been a mega lap, but I lost some time on turn 15 by braking a little late. Still, I couldn't have imagined being on the front row here even last year, so I'm happy. I believe we have the best car, and there's no reason why we can't win.'

Massa, sitting alongside him in the post-qualifying conference, smiled and shook his head. He and Hamilton were good friends off the track, and the Brazilian was not buying into this at all. 'We don't see him as a rookie any more,' he responded. 'We've never seen a guy leading the championship in his first year, so for sure he is no longer a rookie.'

Alonso, meanwhile, was resigned to seeing Hamilton extend his lead at the top of the drivers' championship, as well as the possibility of Massa reducing his nine-point advantage between second and third. 'It's going to be extremely difficult starting from tenth,' Alonso admitted. 'I need points, but

finishing more than fifth in the race is not possible. I will pray for rain during the race all night.'

It was at Magny-Cours that Hamilton wanted to get across another important message. If he ended up becoming champion that season, he wanted to achieve it 'fairly and squarely', a statement that would not have been lost on a watching Michael Schumacher. The competitive German's reign at the top was littered with controversy, as he attempted anything and everything to win races, such as forcing Jacques Villeneuve into the sand in Jerez in 1997, removing Damon Hill in the final race of the 1994 season in Adelaide and parking his car on the circuit in Monaco in 2006 to wreck Alonso's qualifying session.

Hamilton wanted to do it differently. 'It's very important to do it fairly,' he explained. 'How easy it is in golf to drop the ball and say, "There it is." But you're only cheating yourself. It's the same in Formula One. It's such a good feeling to know that you've won fair and square and there have been no nasty moves. That's why I felt even better after Indianapolis when I won, because I knew I'd had a hard but fair battle, and I fought against someone [Alonso] who was a true professional and didn't do anything stupid. It's like a firewall switch in my computer. I would never allow myself to take someone out, because it's just not in my nature.'

At no point did he mention Schumacher by name, but, revealingly, he was keen to praise another legend of his sport, Ayrton Senna, who was also accused of endangering others for his own benefit. Hamilton disagreed. 'I love the whole image of Senna,' he said. 'He was so cool in the car. You could see the lines he was taking, and the moves he made were the best. I also thought he was a very fair driver. People say things about him, but I've seen some of the accidents, and I can't see anything wrong with them. Instead, I see them as ballsy moves, and I'd like to think I could have gone through the same gaps.'

Senna won at Magny-Cours on a good number of occasions, but the French Grand Prix would fail to provide the British driver with a hat-trick of back-to-back victories. Instead, Kimi Räikkönen reminded the world just how good a racing driver he was, and with Massa finishing 2.41 seconds behind him Ferrari recorded their first one–two finish of the season. Hamilton would have to make do with third and an eighth consecutive podium finish in his first eight races in the sport. Kubica matched his fourth place in qualifying with a fourth place in the race, an excellent display from a talented young driver clearly unfazed by his Canadian smash, while Jenson Button finally broke his season's duck with one point garnered from his eighth place. This was just one behind Alonso, who was making life very difficult for himself in his chase for a third world title.

For once, Hamilton's start was not perfect. It was one thing seeing Massa, on pole, race away with a blistering start. It was quite another to see Räikkönen, starting in third place, beat Hamilton to the first corner. It denied Hamilton, carrying a smaller fuel load and thus driving a lighter car, the chance to pull away at the front. After that, Hamilton knew only a superior strategy could win him the race. This time, it failed to materialise for McLaren; Ferrari's tactics were spot on. Coupled with some blisteringly fast laps, Räikkönen was able to steal a march on his colleague to record his first win of the season since the opening Grand Prix in Australia.

'We needed that,' a relieved Räikkönen accepted afterwards. 'It's good to get the win. We are back in the right place. It's a nice feeling, and I think this is the start of our resurgence.'

Hamilton was not too despondent. After all, he had just extended his lead at the top of the drivers' championship to an impressive 14 points. But he was miffed about the first corner. 'I don't like to be overtaken,' he said afterwards. 'It was the first time. It's inevitable, but I'm still on the podium. I think we are the most consistent team, and I've extended my lead, so I'm happy. You can't win every race. What I will say is that I don't think the Ferraris are as fast as they looked. Traffic strategy and being behind them had a lot to do with it, but I still think we can take it to them at Silverstone.'

The British Grand Prix lay in wait in just seven days' time. We were now at the crux of the season, and Lewis Hamilton was returning home as a significant leader in the drivers' championship, but by the time he arrived at the Northamptonshire circuit a far bigger scandal than anyone could recall was starting to brew.

RACE RESULT			
	DRIVER	TEAM	POINTS
1	Kimi Räikkönen	Ferrari	10
2	Felipe Massa	Ferrari	8
3	Lewis Hamilton	McLaren-Mercedes	6
4	Robert Kubica	BMW Sauber	5
5	Nick Heidfeld	BMW Sauber	4
6	Giancarlo Fisichella	Renault	3
7	Fernando Alonso	McLaren-Mercedes	2
8	Jenson Button	Honda	1

CONSTRUCTORS' CHAMPIONSHIP AFTER EIGHT RACES		
	TEAM	POINTS
1	McLaren-Mercedes	114
2	Ferrari	89
3	BMW Sauber	48
4	Renault	28
5	Williams	13
6	Toyota	9
7	Red Bull	6
8	Super Aguri	4
9	Honda	1

DRIVERS' CHAMPIONSHIP AFTER EIGHT RACES		
	DRIVER	POINTS
1	Lewis Hamilton	64
2	Fernando Alonso	50
3	Felipe Massa	47
4	Kimi Räikkönen	42
5	Nick Heidfeld	30
6	Robert Kubica	17
7	Giancarlo Fisichella	16
8	Heikki Kovalainen	12
9	Alex Wurz	8
10	Jarno Trulli	7
11	Nico Rosberg	5
12	David Coulthard	4
12	Takuma Sato	4
14	Mark Webber	2
14	Ralf Schumacher	2
16	Jenson Button	1
16	Sebastian Vettel	1

Race 9

British Grand Prix

Silverstone

Sunday, 8 July 2007

Attendance: 85,000
Weather: dry, 20 °C
Track temperature: 32 °C
Number of laps: 59
Circuit length: 3.194 miles
Race distance: 188.446 miles
Fastest lap: Kimi Räikkönen, 1:20.638 (lap 17)

Hamilton 3rd, 6 points (70)

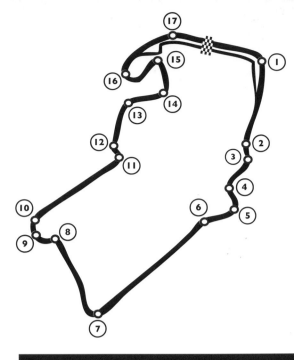

SILVERSTONE CIRCUIT

If Hamilton was disappointed to record 'only' a third place at Magny-Cours, his mood soon brightened as he left France and headed for Silverstone. Only someone with the most ridiculous imagination would have suggested at the start of the season that a young rookie was a good bet to become the first British driver since David Coulthard in 2000 to win the British Grand Prix, but this was the case, regardless of his failure to win in France, as Hamilton arrived with an extensive lead in the drivers' championship.

His childlike excitement – which endeared him even more to the public – was again evident when he considered the next chapter in his extraordinary story. 'To go into your home race in the team you always wanted to drive for and leading the world championship is the greatest feeling a driver can have,' he said. 'It's all pretty unimaginable, isn't it? I keep saying that I didn't expect to finish on the podium so soon, let alone eight times. I'm very proud of myself and the team.'

Those involved with the Silverstone circuit were also rubbing their hands in glee at their unexpected luck. Damon Hill, Britain's last world champion and now president of the British Racing Drivers' Club,

Silverstone's owners, admitted as much. 'It certainly helps us,' he said. 'It's easier to fight for the race if you have a championship leader who is British. It might sound selfish, and I would rather say how excited I am to see someone of his style doing what he is doing.'

Hill had spoken before about his admiration for the kid, but this was increasing as each race passed. 'I'm watching him and trying to work out what his secret is,' he added. 'He's so at ease and charismatic. That's a new thing for Formula One. That's the sort of thing we have seen in motorcycle racing with Valentino Rossi, and other sports, but it's generally been hard to get that across in Formula One. But he's got that.'

He might have added that it was also good to see Ferrari right back in the hunt, not necessarily for Hamilton's world-title aspirations, but in the interests of an epic fight to the finish. A strong test drive at Silverstone bore fruit in France, and now the Italian outfit were gunning for McLaren on their home patch. For Jean Todt, the significance of the French Grand Prix result was not lost. 'The one–two at Magny-Cours was crucial for both championships,' he said.

97

'There are still nine races to go, and everything is still possible. We should try and repeat this result at the home of our main rivals.'

Ron Dennis does not usually need motivating before the British Grand Prix, but with Ferrari throwing down the gauntlet his McLaren team were more eager than usual to redress the balance. 'We will be very strong at Silverstone,' he promised. 'And we're really looking forward to it. Ferrari improved a bit last time, but we did a bad job. This is Formula One. They have had a couple of bad races this year where they flattered us. We flattered them in France. We are not too concerned. Sometimes you have to be pragmatic, take the points and move on to the next race.

'The bottom line is that you're not going to get it right every time. It's good when your drivers admit their mistakes [as Hamilton did concerning turn 15 in qualifying], and we would never criticise either of them, because we make plenty of mistakes on our side. They are driving really well. Fernando drove a fantastic race in France. He was aggressive all the race through. He tried some pretty interesting manoeuvres to try and get people rattled. Two or three came off, others didn't. At the end of the day, he raced from beginning to end.'

His special mention of Alonso smacked a little of trying to appease his increasingly disgruntled star, but if this was a problem that would escalate as the summer went on, it was nothing compared with the 'secrets' scandal that would become a major issue in the days running up to the British Grand Prix and would play a big part in making the 2007 season the most memorable, for reasons both good and bad, for many years.

On the Tuesday prior to race day, it was announced that British engineer Nigel Stepney had been dismissed by Ferrari. Stepney was already suspended and under criminal investigation by an Italian court following a complaint brought against him by his employers. McLaren, meanwhile, discovered that a senior member of their staff was part of the same investigation after he'd allegedly received secret technical information from Stepney in April.

ABOVE: Don't forget to brake! Hamilton flies into the Silverstone pits during the second practice session.

The next day, more news leaked out. Although McLaren refused to name their man, it was revealed to be chief designer Mike Coughlan, one of the sport's most respected and experienced figures. Police had raided his house near the McLaren headquarters in Woking, where it was alleged they found a package containing technical information belonging to Ferrari.

By Thursday, this fast-moving controversy stepped up another gear when the FIA announced that they were monitoring the situation and could quite readily take action. Suddenly, the nightmare scenario became a real possibility. McLaren's involvement – knowingly or unwittingly – could result in serious penalties if they were found to have benefited from the hundreds of pages of confidential information allegedly discovered in Stepney's home. These penalties could include points deductions for both the constructor and its drivers, or even exclusion from the rest of the season.

McLaren moved quickly to protest their innocence. 'We have completed a thorough investigation and can confirm that no Ferrari intellectual property has been passed to any other member of the team or incorporated into the cars,' said a statement. It would be down to the FIA to consider how probable it was that Coughlan did not put the technical information provided by Stepney to good use with McLaren. Ferrari were certainly not prepared to let the issue go. They reacted to McLaren's statement by issuing one of their own, stating that they 'reserve the right to consider all implications, be they criminal, civil or of any other nature'.

Hamilton refused to get into the issue with four days to go before the race. Instead, he focused on trying to win the British Grand Prix. 'To win at this race would be immense,' he said. 'But we have to be realistic with our expectations. Without a doubt, it will be the biggest race of the year for me, as it's my debut home race. It's going to be another new experience. I expect the atmosphere will be incredible, and I cannot wait to race in front of my home fans. I'll do my best for them.'

By the Friday, a third team had joined the 'espionage' party, and for a while this was good news to a wounded McLaren team whose integrity had been questioned by the whole sorry affair. Late in the afternoon, Honda issued a statement that read, 'Given the speculation surrounding the legal investigations at Ferrari and McLaren, the Honda Racing Formula One team would like to clarify that earlier this year Nigel Stepney, formerly of Ferrari, requested a meeting with Nick Fry, CEO of the Honda Racing Formula One team. Stepney subsequently met in June with Nick Fry and brought with him Mike Coughlan of McLaren with a view to investigating job opportunities within the Honda Racing Formula One team. At no point was any confidential information offered or received. Nick Fry informed Jean Todt and Ron Dennis of the meeting and has offered to provide any information required by Ferrari and McLaren.'

Dennis was visibly upset about the suggestion in some quarters that McLaren as a team had played

some part in all of this. 'What I've learned more than anything over the last few days is how fast people are prepared to jump into severe criticism of McLaren,' he said. 'Too many people are quick to criticise and condemn. The truth will come out.'

Meanwhile, his drivers had a job to do and an increasingly serious one now that Ferrari appeared to be back in business. Up until then, Hamilton had revealed just how talented and confident a driver he was, despite his inexperience and age. At Silverstone, another characteristic was revealed: his showmanship. And the crowd who turned up in their tens of thousands clearly appreciated it when the rookie snatched pole position right from under Kimi Räikkönen's nose with a final flying lap with just 30 seconds of qualifying remaining. He was only lying in fourth place as the seconds devoured the final minute of the third and last qualifying session,

behind Räikkönen, Alonso and Massa. Appearing remarkably unperturbed for a young man on his debut British Grand Prix, he sat patiently in the pits as his crew changed his tyres before blasting out onto the Silverstone circuit to nudge the Finn into second place on the grid by a tenth of a second. 'It was all down to that last lap,' he admitted afterwards. 'I did a sweet job.'

As the news flashed up on giant screens dotted all around the Northamptonshire circuit, a huge roar was heard from the 80,000 crowd, most of whom had come to see the new British sensation of Formula One, judging by the waving of Union Jacks adorned with Hamilton's name. This figure smashed the previous record for qualifying day at the British Grand Prix by a staggering 12,000. It was 2,000 more

ABOVE: An impatient Hamilton is about to leave the pits prematurely, midway through the British Grand Prix.

than the number who turned up to see the actual race the previous year and just 5,000 fewer than the capacity crowd figure at Silverstone of 85,000. A sell-out crowd would be expected the following day, and it was nearly all down to one man. Lewismania, it seemed, was now official.

Hamilton screamed with delight for the whole of his lap of honour and shook his fist in triumph to the waving hordes of his new fans. At the same time, Anthony went berserk in the pit lane, jumping, shouting in joy and waving almost uncontrollably to anyone and everyone, while Nicholas also joined in the wild family celebrations.

It had been seven years since Coulthard's race victory at Silverstone and eleven since Damon Hill was the last British driver to claim pole at the British Grand Prix. Neither of them received the kind of response Hamilton experienced after qualifying. Indeed, you had to go back to the days of Nigel Mansell to remember a time when such scenes had been witnessed before. Now Hamilton had clinched pole – the 50th for the McLaren-Mercedes partnership – in the one race that meant more to him than any other. 'I've never had to dig so deep as I did for that last lap,' Hamilton explained, his voice hoarse after shouting out the word 'yes' for the whole of the 3.194-mile circuit. 'I hadn't been quick enough in previous laps, and I'd been struggling a bit. I knew I was in fourth place, but I also knew, even with thirty seconds remaining, that there was plenty of time for one last attempt. This is what racing is all about. I was on a knife-edge during that last lap. I realised that one small error would blow it. You can't imagine the pressure I put on myself knowing that it was all coming down to one last lap. Put simply, I realised that I had to be faster at every single corner of the lap. When I knew I'd got pole, it was a phenomenal feeling, as good as when I won my first Grand Prix in Canada last month. I made sure the radio was switched off and then screamed "yes" for the whole of the next lap. I was screaming as loud as the fans. Now I'm really looking forward to tomorrow. I'm going to do the best job I can.'

Räikkönen, who was still lying fourth in the drivers' championship despite his win in France, had to settle for second place on the grid after a mistake at the final turn of the lap saw him veer out wide. 'I ran off the track at the last exit, and that's disappointing,' said the Finn. 'I definitely had pole until then, but I can still win the race.'

Alonso's bid to narrow the gap with his rookie teammate at the top of the drivers' championship took another knock when he could only record the third-fastest time. 'I know what I'm capable of doing, and I still hope to be able to do it,' he insisted later. 'But I realise it's going to be very difficult to catch Lewis.'

That night, Hamilton was in a reflective and indeed religious mood. A devout Christian, he put much of

his astounding success down to his faith. 'My faith is very important to me,' he explained. 'I'm a true believer. I really believe that my talent is God-given and that I've been truly blessed. I guess every driver is talented, but some of us are prepared to work harder to make the most of our talent. Some don't possess the talent of someone like Kimi Räikkönen, but they've worked harder to become better than him. I don't

ABOVE: Who's the local favourite at Silverstone? No prizes for guessing that most people wanted Hamilton to win the British Grand Prix.

know if I've worked harder than Fernando Alonso, but I do know I've worked very hard.'

Another legend of the sport became a member of the Lewis Hamilton fan club that weekend at Silverstone, a man who knew all about inter-team rivalries between two major talents. Alain Prost, the four-time world champion, used to drive for McLaren, and although he enjoyed much success there his time was as much remembered for his intense, often acrimonious rivalry with his teammate Ayrton Senna. 'I love a human story in motor racing, and we have one this year, for sure,' he said. 'The fight between two drivers in the same team, one a youngster new to Formula One and the other slightly older, more experienced and twice the world champion, makes it exceptional.

'I can understand just how Fernando must feel. When Ayrton came to McLaren, he was the new guy who everyone wanted. It's the same now with Hamilton. Fernando really wanted to go to McLaren. He had all these ideas of going there as world champion. But once he got there, I think he found it was not like his dreams. In fact, he got there and found out he is not even the number one when the other driver is a rookie. He did not expect Lewis to be so quick, either. From the first race, I could see that Alonso was not driving the car the same way as Hamilton. Lewis is really driving the car perfectly. Alonso, though, is driving too aggressively. He is fighting to find the speed. Lewis is just there with it. What I like most about Lewis is his attitude. His approach is the best one to have. He seems to possess the whole package. He is the best newcomer the sport has ever seen. Just think, when he's 25 years old he's going to be unimaginably good.'

And so they came to crown a prince at Silverstone, not only the die-hard Formula One fans, but celebrity royalty, too, led by David and Victoria Beckham. However, from the rookie's perspective, an old man in the crowd was the most welcome spectator. Davidson Hamilton, Lewis's grandfather, had flown over from Grenada to watch his grandson in a Formula One race for the first time. They had all come to see Hamilton's far-fetched story become a little more unlikely, but they would be disappointed. Despite starting on pole, Hamilton could only finish a distant third behind second-placed Alonso and the winner Kimi Räikkönen, who made it back-to-back wins after his success in France the previous

week and 12 career Formula One Grand Prix wins in total.

Despite his pole, observers in the paddock knew that Ferrari were flying and Räikkönen, in particular, would be hard to keep down. So it transpired, although Hamilton's start was made at its usual electrifying rate to ensure he reached the first corner, at a speed of 185 mph, with his nose ahead of the Finn's. The lead was thus his, but he could not extend it over the next 16 laps as the Ferrari was all over him from behind. It might have been worse, too, if Massa had not stalled on the starting grid.

It was during his first pit stop that Hamilton finally made his first obvious mistake. Whether through anxiety or overeagerness, he dashed out of his area before the lollipop had been lifted to confirm the all-clear. With the fuel pipe still attached, this cost him a couple of seconds. Two laps later, Räikkönen made his first pit stop and surrendered the lead to Alonso. Yet the outcome of the race was decided as a result of the second pit stop. Alonso went first, but Räikkönen lapped the circuit so quickly that when he also dived into the pits he emerged three seconds in front of the world champion. That was that. The Finn tore away to win again, Alonso finished runner-up and Hamilton came third, his ninth consecutive podium placing, but almost 40 seconds behind the winner. Robert Kubica's impressive debut season in Formula One – a rookie overshadowed by Hamilton but enjoying a tremendous first season in his own right – continued with a fourth and Massa, who had to start the race in the pit lane, tore through the field like a man possessed to record a fifth placing.

It was now evident that the battle for the world drivers' title had become a four-way tussle and the fight for the constructors' title a two-horse race. Räikkönen, never one to go overboard with celebrations, was nonetheless happy with his day's work. 'This is important,' he said. 'The car is better for me now. It is still a long season, and we will keep on pushing.'

Hamilton was honest enough to accept blame for his mistake in the pit lane that contributed to his third-place finish. 'I selected first gear and was ready to go,' he explained. 'I thought I saw the lollipop move a little bit, but I was maybe wrong, and I let the clutch

FACING PAGE: The Hamilton factor at work – even David and Victoria Beckham are lured to Silverstone by the rookie.

out too early. You try to be as quick as you can when the lollipop goes up. I tried to anticipate it and messed up. It lost me a lot of valuable time, and I then had to push, but I struggled with the balance. I need to step up my game, and I intend to do so.

'I made the wrong decision with set-up, and it really caused me problems during the race. Even in qualifying, I didn't have the pace I should have had, but it was too late by then to change the car, so I've learned a good lesson. We've come away with a ninth podium position. I'm the most consistent driver here. I think you have to be happy with that.'

Anthony took the realistic view as well. 'It's disappointing, but if this is the worst disappointment, I'll take it,' he said. 'Winning the British Grand Prix would have been the icing on the cake, but it's good to learn there are downs as well as ups.'

Still, these were interesting times for McLaren and Lewis Hamilton. They had a High Court hearing the following Tuesday in London to investigate the controversy surrounding the leaked documents between Ferrari and McLaren, and Fernando Alonso was beginning to believe that the pendulum was about to swing his way again.

RACE RESULT

	DRIVER	TEAM	POINTS
1	Kimi Räikkönen	Ferrari	10
2	Fernando Alonso	McLaren-Mercedes	8
3	Lewis Hamilton	McLaren-Mercedes	6
4	Robert Kubica	BMW Sauber	5
5	Felipe Massa	Ferrari	4
6	Nick Heidfeld	BMW Sauber	3
7	Heikki Kovalainen	Renault	2
8	Giancarlo Fisichella	Renault	1

CONSTRUCTORS' CHAMPIONSHIP AFTER NINE RACES

	TEAM	POINTS
1	McLaren-Mercedes	128
2	Ferrari	103
3	BMW Sauber	56
4	Renault	31
5	Williams	13
6	Toyota	9
7	Red Bull	6
8	Super Aguri	4
9	Honda	1

DRIVERS' CHAMPIONSHIP AFTER NINE RACES

	DRIVER	POINTS
1	Lewis Hamilton	70
2	Fernando Alonso	58
3	Kimi Räikkönen	52
4	Felipe Massa	51
5	Nick Heidfeld	33
6	Robert Kubica	22
7	Giancarlo Fisichella	17
8	Heikki Kovalainen	14
9	Alex Wurz	8
10	Jarno Trulli	7
11	Nico Rosberg	5
12	David Coulthard	4
12	Takuma Sato	4
14	Mark Webber	2
14	Ralf Schumacher	2
16	Jenson Button	1
16	Sebastian Vettel	1

FACING PAGE: A disappointing podium? He wanted to win it, but Hamilton had to settle for third at Silverstone.

Race 10

European Grand Prix

Nürburg

Sunday, 22 July 2007

Attendance: 125,000
Weather: wet/dry, 19 °C
Track temperature: 30 °C
Number of laps: 60
Circuit length: 3.199 miles
Race distance: 191.94 miles
Fastest lap: Felipe Massa, 1:32.853 (lap 34)

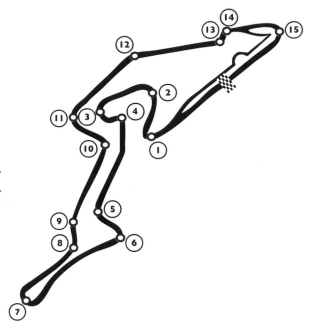

NÜRBURGRING

Hamilton 9th, 0 points (70)

Fernando Alonso was smiling again. After trailing behind Hamilton for much of the season, the world champion sensed his better placing at the British Grand Prix was the start of his comeback, and he was more than happy to make this point. On the day that McLaren's Mike Coughlan was implicated in a High Court case over the spying scandal engulfing the sport, the Spaniard was more concerned about the defence of his title.

'Sooner or later, I will close the gap,' he promised, Hamilton's lead having been reduced by two points to twelve. 'Since Canada, I have been quite a bit faster than him. At Indianapolis, I couldn't overtake him, and at Magny-Cours I had that gearbox problem. Here we had a normal race, and I finished more than 30 seconds in front of him. There are favourable races coming up now, like Germany and Hungary, and the target is to finish ahead of Hamilton. From now on, I must always be on the podium, and always a step higher than him.'

Alonso may not have been concerned about the espionage allegations, but McLaren certainly were, especially after the FIA decided to charge them with a breach of the International Sporting Code. The team were ordered to appear before the FIA's World Motor Sport Council in Paris four days after the next race, the European Grand Prix at the Nürburgring. The key regulation under scrutiny was article 151c, which dealt with 'any fraudulent conduct or any act prejudicial to the interests of any competition or to the interests of motor sport generally'.

In a statement, the FIA said, 'The team representatives have been called to answer a charge that between March and July 2007, in breach of article 151c of the International Sporting Code, Vodafone McLaren-Mercedes had unauthorised possession of documents and confidential information belonging to Scuderia Ferrari Marlboro, including information that could be used to design, engineer, build, check, test, develop and/or run a 2007 Ferrari Formula One car.'

McLaren responded with their own statement. 'McLaren is extremely disappointed to note that it has been asked by the FIA to answer a charge of being in possession of certain documents and confidential information belonging to Ferrari,' it said. 'Whilst McLaren wishes to continue its full cooperation with any investigation into this matter, it does wish to make it very clear that the documents and confidential information were only in the possession of one currently suspended employee on an unauthorised basis, and no element of it has been used in relation to McLaren's Formula One cars.' Nevertheless, the potential penalties available to the FIA could range from fines to the expulsion from that season's championship of both the team and its drivers if it could be proved that the information acquired by Coughlan was useful to McLaren. There was a sudden and real danger that all of Hamilton's first-season achievements could be wiped from the slate. The FIA, moreover, had a record of meting out drastic measures, while president Max Mosley made a point of suggesting that it was rare for a team to be punished without its drivers also suffering. 'The credibility of Formula One and sporting fairness is at stake,' Mosley said. A FIA spokesman added, 'We don't call an emergency meeting of the World Motor Sport Council lightly. We cannot rule out the fact that any sanction against the team would have implications for the drivers.'

Hamilton had kept his own counsel on this rapidly increasing scandal, at least until he arrived at the famous Nürburgring. 'I've only been with the Formula One team a year, but I have known Ron nine years, and this is something he would never do,' he insisted to a gathering of the world's media. 'That's why I have such great belief in the team. There are always teams trying to bend the rules in some way, but I honestly believe we are the most honest. For me, I believe we will be all right. I don't think the drivers will be docked points, and so it really isn't playing on my mind at all.'

Hamilton started his campaign at the European Grand Prix bunged up with flu but remained, nonetheless, upbeat and recognised the fact that he was now there to be shot at. 'For sure, I am the target,' he accepted. 'I always have been. I still approach things the same way. You've got to focus. It gets harder to maintain the level of performance. The person who is the most consistent is the person who will do it.' Despite his championship lead, he refused to nominate himself as favourite to win the world title. 'I don't see myself as favourite,' he said. 'I never go into a season, or go through it, believing that. I have my own set of beliefs, and I know what I can do, but that's for me to keep to myself. If we win, then that's fantastic. It's great for the team, and great for me and my career,

which, of course, we are all working towards. If not, then we just hope for the best.'

Part of the reason why Hamilton appeared to be so positive was what had happened at testing in Spa-Francorchamps in Belgium the week before the European Grand Prix. Set-up issues prevented him from making the most of his pole position at Silverstone, but Hamilton, boosted by a powerful

ABOVE: Hamilton squeezes every last drop out of his McLaren-Mercedes during qualifying at the Nürburgring.

performance in the Belgian forests, felt these were now in the past. 'Spa was great for me,' he insisted. 'It gave me such a boost. The car felt great again. I'm all set.'

To prove his point, he went on to clock the fastest time during Friday's free practice for the European Grand Prix, some 0.2 seconds faster than Kimi Räikkönen and 0.4 seconds quicker than Fernando Alonso. In the afternoon, Hamilton twice spun off the circuit, which would prove to be a portent of what was to come. 'The first time, I was carrying too much speed into the corner and trying to find my limits,' he explained. 'The next time I think it was because I damaged a tyre.'

Still, he woke up on the Saturday morning in a confident mood after his free practice exertions, and he was also far more relaxed at a circuit at which he had won twice in GP2 the year before than at Silverstone, where he had been very much the centre of attention. 'It's more relaxed here,' he confirmed. 'That's good to see. Silverstone was incredible. I have never seen anything like it, not even in previous years watching Formula One. When you are at the centre of attention and it's manic, it's difficult to cope. As for here, anything is a bonus. I'm still going through the season not expecting to win the world title. If I don't, then that's racing, and it was to be expected coming into the season. If we do, then I'll be very, very happy.'

He would also have been happy to have heard what Murray Walker had to say about him. Walker, the legendary voice of Formula One, was coming out of retirement to commentate for BBC Radio Five Live as a one-off and was delighted to assess Hamilton in a more than favourable light. 'Lewis can potentially blow Michael Schumacher away and become the greatest of all time,' insisted the 83 year old. 'I'm not denigrating Schumacher, but he was in a position where the second driver had to defer to him. Lewis is up against a double world champion, Fernando Alonso, in his own team, up against Kimi Räikkönen, who's bloody good, and Felipe Massa, who's bloody good as well. And the BMWs and Renaults aren't exactly hanging about. It's all capped by the fact that he's such a nice bloke: humble, dignified, cheerful, eloquent, pleasant. If you could write the CV for an ideal Grand Prix driver, it would be like his.'

However, the Saturday would mark the start of Hamilton's worst race weekend to date in Formula One. It began with a crash that at first appeared to be horrific. During qualifying, he smashed his McLaren into a tyre wall, and his front-right wheel came loose, forcing the car to veer off at the end of the fast straight at turn eight. Ironically, he had just set the fastest split time through the circuit's first sector of three. For a while, onlookers almost feared the worst. Hamilton sat in his wrecked car for at least a couple of minutes, his legs shaking visibly, before being aided from the cockpit by marshals and then collapsing, dramatically, on the ground.

Trackside medics attended to him for nearly a quarter of an hour before he was lifted into the back of an ambulance, his neck in a brace and with a drip attached. Although Hamilton attempted to be brave, smiling weakly and giving a thumbs-up sign, he was taken to the Nürburgring medical centre. While the world waited for further news, Ron Dennis spoke of his serious concern. 'The most disturbing thing was that we couldn't speak to him,' he said. 'It took 30 to 45 seconds to realise that the impact had caused the radio to fail, and in that period there was no dialogue and no reassurance of him saying, "I'm fine". Also, the in-car camera position showing him exercising his legs was quite alarming. You don't know if he was doing that as a result of pain or some other problem.'

The signs were ominous when Hamilton was subsequently airlifted by helicopter to a military hospital in Koblenz, some twenty-five miles away, for a CT scan, but he returned to the paddock two hours later and casually walked into the McLaren motorhome. Unable to continue with qualifying, which had long finished, Hamilton would be starting the European Grand Prix in tenth place, his lowest position on the grid, providing he came through a final examination in the morning with FIA medical delegate Gary Hartstein.

'I'm very fortunate that I haven't got any bruises, although I'm sure I'll wake up with some tomorrow,' he reassured everyone. 'The most important thing is that I'm OK, and the team are doing a good job to make sure we have a decent car for tomorrow. Ron says I have to be signed off tomorrow morning, so we'll have to wait and see. But I feel fine for the race, so fingers crossed.'

A clearly relieved Dennis added, 'He is absolutely fine, and at this moment there is no medical reason why he can't race. The procedure is that he'll have a night's sleep and a final check in the morning. He has no bruising and no damage anywhere. It was only when I got to the medical centre that I had a clear understanding of how he was, though. We got a report from the medical team that he was conscious and stable, but that doesn't really convey much. It was pretty distressing until the point I knew he was actually fine. The first thing Lewis said to me when I saw him was, "I want to race."'

The crash had happened with just five minutes of

FACING PAGE: Hamilton scare – Lewis is stretchered off the circuit on a drip after crashing in qualifying at the European Grand Prix. Amazingly, he raced the next day.

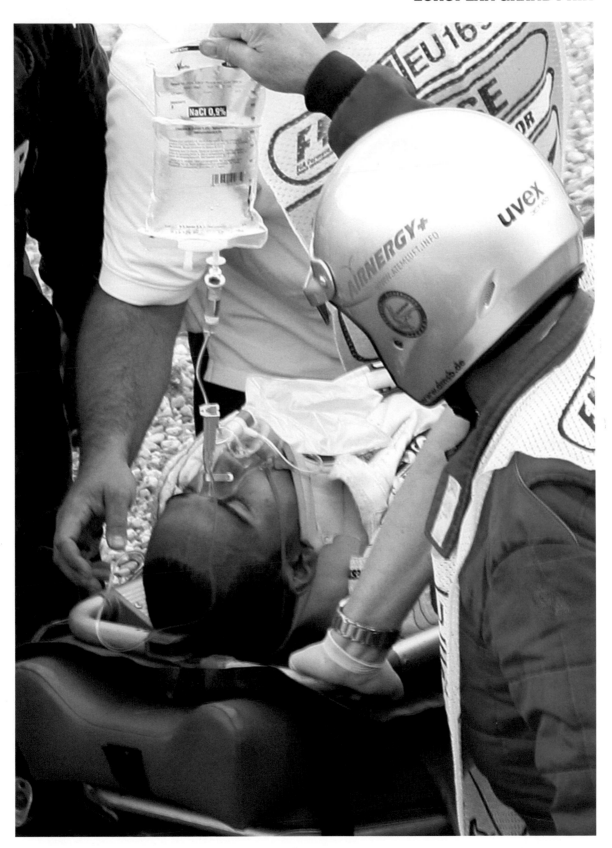

ABOVE: Two's company, three's a crowd – Dennis and Hamilton walk through the spacious McLaren motorhome in Germany.

qualifying remaining, forcing a half-hour delay in the proceedings. The red flag was waved, qualifying was suspended, Hamilton's car was removed by a crane and the tyre wall was rebuilt. And in Hamilton's absence, his three closest rivals made the most of it, with Kimi Räikkönen grabbing pole, Fernando Alonso securing second place on the grid and Felipe Massa third. A faulty wheel gun was later blamed for the accident – it had not secured the tyre well enough. The vibration caused by the poorly fitted rubber

forced it to burst and send Hamilton hurtling across sand and into the barrier.

'The wheel wasn't put on properly,' Dennis explained. 'But that's not the mechanic's fault. We're not quite sure what failed, but it was quite fortunate, because the same gun was used on Fernando's car, and he hadn't started to lean on it yet. We could therefore tell that it was a gun failure. Our telemetry shows that the deflation was absolutely instantaneous. At least we know we don't have a problem with the car. The team will be undertaking a full investigation to understand how this could have happened.' Although this was Hamilton's third accident since he had received the nod to drive the McLaren in November 2006 – he had a 160-mph crash during testing in Valencia in January and a 140-mph accident in practice for the Monaco Grand Prix in May – the repercussions, in terms of the drivers' championship, could prove to be more serious.

'The lap was going really well, and then, all of a sudden, I went up to turn eight and something just happened,' Hamilton recalled. 'I lost grip and went straight on. At that point, you're just a passenger, so you just hold on for dear life, and when you hit the wall you hope it's not painful. But it was very painful in my chest and legs. I waited for a while before I got out of the car. Eventually, I was able to climb out, but then I had problems with my legs. I think that with the shock I couldn't stand up. I was conscious. I was just in pain with my chest, and I had this big bruise. Thanks to the medical team for doing such a great job. I wanted to race. Even when I got out, I

was asking the medical team, "How badly damaged is my car?"'

Alonso got lucky in a big way. The Spaniard was out on the track when Hamilton crashed and about to embark on a flying lap when the session was stopped. When he returned to the pits, he discovered that he also had a loose front-right wheel nut, which had been fitted by the same air gun that had failed Hamilton. The problem was sorted out, and Alonso was able to return to the track when the session began again 30 minutes later to claim a secondary position on the front row of the grid. 'The best news about today is that Lewis is OK,' he added.

The best news about the next day for Alonso was that he won the European Grand Prix, while Hamilton's weekend of disasters continued. He

BELOW: T-Car technicians – McLaren mechanics go to work on the T-Car after Hamilton's big crash at the Nürburgring.

ABOVE: Wish I had windscreen wipers – Hamilton slips and slides his way to a disappointing ninth place in Germany.

completed the race – somehow – but his ninth placing not only put an end to his incredible run of nine consecutive podiums in his first nine races but also meant that because he had scored no points, as opposed to Alonso's maximum, the Spaniard would end the day just two points behind the twenty-two-year-old Briton in the drivers' championship.

The race began well enough for Hamilton. By the very first corner, he had already leapt from tenth to sixth and by the second corner to fourth, taking advantage of Nick Heidfeld and Robert Kubica's BMWs colliding into one other. This vastly improved position for Hamilton would only last a few seconds longer, however. Within seconds, his back-left tyre was punctured by debris from the BMWs.

Even before the first lap had been concluded, more drama had occurred. A sudden and heavy downpour of rain engulfed the circuit, forcing all but one of the cars to dash into the pits to change their tyres to wets. The lone car left remaining on the circuit belonged to Spyker's German rookie Markus Winkelhock, who remarkably found himself leading the race after his boss Mike Gascoyne had decided to bring him back to the pits during the parade lap to switch rubbers. A hydraulic problem would later end his race.

With streams of water running in torrents across the track, Jenson Button, Nico Rosberg, Adrian Sutil, Scott Speed, Vitantonio Liuzzi and Hamilton all flew off the circuit at turn one on the third lap, with only Hamilton rejoining the race after a crane winched him out of the gravel and back onto the circuit. The safety car emerged, but by lap four the driving conditions had become so absurdly difficult that the race was stopped for what turned out to be twenty-two minutes.

The cars returned to the grid, lined up and waited to start again. Hamilton, a lap behind, started in 17th place and immediately took a gamble by changing to dry tyres on lap six, despite the slippery conditions. It did not result in a points finish, but at least he was able to remind race goers just what an exciting driver he was, twice overtaking Giancarlo Fisichella and Rubens Barrichello before claiming a disappointing ninth-place finish.

Further up the field, Alonso won the race and Massa was second. However, they became entwined in

ABOVE: Hamilton, Scott Speed and Jenson Button all come a cropper in the Nürburgring gravel, with only Hamilton able to continue.

a finger-jabbing argument as soon as they stepped out of their cars at the finish after they had come together on turn five when the Spaniard had claimed the inside line. The exchange remained heated as they entered the weighing room, with both arguing their case in Italian and Alonso accusing the Brazilian of driving into him. He would later retract this accusation and apologise, no doubt comforted by the enormously successful day he had just experienced. Not only had he reduced Hamilton's twelve-point lead to just two, but with Kimi Räikkönen retiring on the 35th lap the Finn now lay sixteen points behind him and eighteen behind Hamilton. Red Bull's Mark Webber claimed a surprise third place in the race, the team's first appearance on the podium since the 2006 Monaco Grand Prix. And Alex Wurz brought some joy to the Williams team by coming home fourth.

'This is more than a win,' said a delighted Alonso later. 'This is ten points to Lewis and Kimi, and two to Massa. The championship is wide open. I would not put money on anyone to win. It was a crazy race, especially with the rain. At one stage, cars were aquaplaning everywhere.'

Hamilton was still fighting after the race. 'I never gave up,' he pointed out. 'I pushed to the very end. The FIA made me back off when Felipe was four seconds behind and I was faster than him. It was the same with Fernando. Overall, I must have lost ten seconds. Without that I would have scored some points.

'I said from day one that there would be a time when I would not be on the podium. This weekend I have learned 100 per cent more than normal. I came here completely sick, had one of the biggest crashes ever, then had a puncture and went into the gravel again as heavy rain fell, but I'm thrilled that I've taken a big step in my development. I learned ten times as much today. I've probably had less than 500 km in the wet, for example, which is hardly anything at all. I hope this is the one weekend when things go wrong. I'm still positive, and I'm still leading the championship. There are seven races left. That's a long way to go, and I had more fun today than in the past nine races.'

Even after the weekend he had just experienced, Lewis Hamilton's unshakeable confidence remained untouched. He would need it to remain that way as Fernando Alonso continued to up the ante.

FACING PAGE: Fancy seeing you here! Alonso jokes with a delighted Mark Webber, who claims an unlikely third place on the Nürburgring podium.

RACE RESULT

	DRIVER	TEAM	POINTS
1	Fernando Alonso	McLaren-Mercedes	10
2	Felipe Massa	Ferrari	8
3	Mark Webber	Red Bull	6
4	Alex Wurz	Williams	5
5	David Coulthard	Red Bull	4
6	Nick Heidfeld	BMW Sauber	3
7	Robert Kubica	BMW Sauber	2
8	Heikki Kovalainen	Renault	1

CONSTRUCTORS' CHAMPIONSHIP AFTER TEN RACES

	TEAM	POINTS
1	McLaren-Mercedes	138
2	Ferrari	111
3	BMW Sauber	61
4	Renault	32
5	Williams	18
6	Red Bull	16
7	Toyota	9
8	Super Aguri	4
9	Honda	1

DRIVERS' CHAMPIONSHIP AFTER TEN RACES

	DRIVER	POINTS
1	Lewis Hamilton	70
2	Fernando Alonso	68
3	Felipe Massa	59
4	Kimi Räikkönen	52
5	Nick Heidfeld	36
6	Robert Kubica	24
7	Giancarlo Fisichella	17
8	Heikki Kovalainen	15
9	Alex Wurz	13
10	David Coulthard	8
10	Mark Webber	8
12	Jarno Trulli	7
13	Nico Rosberg	5
14	Takuma Sato	4
15	Ralf Schumacher	2
16	Jenson Button	1
16	Sebastian Vettel	1

Race 11

Hungarian Grand Prix

Budapest

Sunday, 5 August 2007

Attendance: 78,000
Weather: sunny, 31 °C
Track temperature: 43 °C
Number of laps: 70
Circuit length: 2.722 miles
Race distance: 190.54 miles
Fastest lap: Kimi Räikkönen, 1:20.047 (lap 70)

Hamilton 1st, 10 points (80)

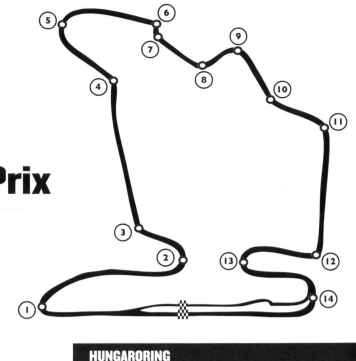

HUNGARORING

After a six-hour hearing at the Paris headquarters of the FIA, McLaren were given a conditional pardon in the 'Ferrari-gate' affair, and there was relief all round, from owner Ron Dennis to drivers Lewis Hamilton and Fernando Alonso. The FIA would now focus their attention on Nigel Stepney, the sacked Ferrari engineer, and Michael Coughlan, McLaren chief designer, who were to be summoned to the French capital for further questioning.

In simple terms, the FIA acknowledged that McLaren had indeed contravened article 151c of the International Sporting Code but decided that there was insufficient evidence to warrant a points deduction or fine. If the team had been found guilty of benefiting from the confidential Ferrari documentation, then the drivers, and McLaren, would have faced expulsion from the competition. The threat of such dramatic action would continue to hang over the team, however, for the next 18 months, coming into effect if further evidence came to light. The FIA statement read, 'The World Motor Sport Council are satisfied that Vodafone McLaren-Mercedes were in possession of confidential Ferrari information and, therefore, in breach of article 151c

of the International Sporting Code. However, there is insufficient evidence that this information was used in such a way as to interfere improperly with the FIA Formula One world championship. We, therefore, impose no penalty.'

Dennis was understandably relieved when he emerged from the hearing, although he was still slightly concerned by the continuing threat of expulsion. 'The process has been long and detailed,' he admitted. 'I'm not completely comfortable with the outcome. Moving forward, McLaren want to reaffirm our long-standing commitment to honesty and integrity, and restate that we have acted correctly throughout. Now we have a Formula One world championship to win. As a result, we intend to move on, so as to maintain the focus and commitment required to do exactly that.'

Hamilton, who had posted the fastest times in testing that week in Jerez, was happy in the knowledge that his bid to become the first rookie to win a world title would continue unabated. 'While it's only my first season in Formula One with the team, I already know and appreciate the commitment and dedication of the people here,' he said. 'As a result,

I am pleased with today's decision and can't wait for the rest of the season.'

Ferrari, in contrast, were astounded by the governing body's verdict. 'Ferrari . . . find it incomprehensible that violating the fundamental principle of sporting honesty does not have, as a logical and inevitable consequence, the application of a sanction,' said a Ferrari statement. 'Today's decision legitimises dishonest behaviour in Formula One and sets a very serious precedent. The decision of the world council signifies that possession and knowledge at the very highest level of highly confidential information acquired in an illicit manner, and the acquiring of confidential information over the course of several months, represent violations which do not carry any punishment. The fact McLaren were in possession of such information was discovered totally by accident, and but for this the team would continue to have it. Ferrari feels that this is highly prejudicial to the credibility of the sport. We will continue with the legal action under way within the Italian criminal justice system and in the civil court in England.'

It was a promise that would later deliver a fatal blow to McLaren-Mercedes, but not Lewis Hamilton or his teammate Alonso. The process began when the FIA granted an appeal against the decision reached the week before by the World Motor Sport Council. The second hearing was granted following a challenge by the Automobile Club of Italy (ACI) on behalf of Ferrari, their licence holder. Quite clearly, this posed a bigger threat, because the appeal would allow Ferrari's lawyers to cross-examine McLaren and present new evidence to the court, unlike at the World Council hearing.

In reply to the ACI, Max Mosley, the FIA president, said, 'Your letter suggests that the outcome may have been different if the council had given Ferrari further opportunities to be heard beyond those that were offered. Because of this, and the importance of public confidence in the outcome, I will send this matter to the FIA Court of Appeal.' If incriminating evidence was revealed in this later hearing condemning McLaren, then the FIA would have little option but to issue expulsions.

It was with all this hanging over him that Hamilton made the journey to Budapest and the Hungaroring circuit for race 11 of the 17-race Formula One season. This would be a true test of his racing worth,

following his worst performance of the season to date at the Nürburgring a fortnight earlier.

The Hungaroring is renowned as one of the most gruelling venues on the Formula One circuit, with a short pit straight and 14 corners that make overtaking difficult. Only the Monaco Grand Prix has slower lap times, and drivers are taught not to stray too far from the established racing lines, because the arid conditions result in a great deal of dust being deposited on the circuit. The year before in GP2 Hamilton crashed before he was able to set a qualifying time and had to start the first race at the back of the grid in twenty-sixth and last place. He showed his racing appetite by finishing in tenth, and then followed that up with a second place in the second race of the weekend.

The testing session at Jerez showed everyone that a ninth place at the European Grand Prix had not dented Hamilton's confidence or form. Even when he ended Friday's free practice session in the gravel trap, he was happy with his prospects. 'I've always seen myself as the rookie of the championship, and I'm learning all the way,' Hamilton said. 'I'm leading the world championship, but I don't feel there is too much pressure. I have Fernando breathing heavily down my neck, but that is not too much of a worry. I think I have as good a chance as anyone. I came away from the last race with a smile on my face. Yes, I lost ten points, but I learned so much. I also reminded myself in the race that you never give up.'

If his demeanour appeared relaxed and happy on the Friday night, it would change dramatically inside the next 24 hours. By Saturday evening, Hamilton's lot had risen dramatically and controversially when his uneasy relationship with Fernando suddenly took a dramatic dive as civil war broke out in the McLaren camp. Hamilton believed, quite rightly, that he had been denied pole position in qualifying after he had been unable to complete his flying lap because the Spaniard had delayed his exit from the pit lane, thus blocking his teammate until he had run out of time to initiate the final lap. The incident led to a furious exchange of words between Hamilton and his mentor Ron Dennis, although reports that the rookie used the f-word at his boss over the car radio were later strenuously denied. Then, just before midnight, race stewards demoted Alonso five places down the grid as a result of his actions, promoting

FACING PAGE: Don't mess with me! FIA president Max Mosley.

Hamilton from second to first and presenting him with a golden opportunity to extend his lead in the drivers' championship. McLaren were hit hard, too, by being refused the chance to score any points in the constructors' title race as a result of Alonso's actions.

It took seven hours of deliberation before the three independent stewards delivered their verdict at 11.35 p.m. In a statement, they said, 'The actions of the team in the final qualifying session are considered prejudicial to the interests of the competition and to the interest of motor sport generally.'

That was pretty evident, based on what a disbelieving world had witnessed that afternoon. Alonso remained stationary in his car for ten seconds in the pits, despite the lollipop being raised to signal that he could leave, with Hamilton left stranded behind him, waiting to change his tyres and set off for a final flying lap. When Alonso finally departed, there was exactly one second remaining, which was time enough for Alonso, but not his furious teammate. The deliberate hold-up ensured that the rookie did not have enough time to complete the lap and improve on his previous fastest time, which Alonso went on to better by a tenth of a second, taking what he believed to be pole. Hamilton had been easily the quickest in the first two qualifying sessions, so it was a fair bet that he would have come through in that final attempt.

'I really don't know why I was held back,' said Hamilton after qualifying was officially over, quite clearly angry about what had just taken place. 'I guess you should ask the team, and I definitely will when I go back and have a debrief. It will need a good explanation.' This had clearly not been given to him when Hamilton, alongside Dennis and Alonso, faced the media one hour later. 'I was obviously told on the way in that Fernando was doing his stop and that I should back off so I didn't have to queue,' he said. 'That's what I did, so I saved some time coming round the last corner and into the pits. But, for some reason, he just held there.' He was then asked how much more time he would have required to have been able to cross the start–finish line and begin his flying lap. 'About the same amount of time that I was held up in the pit stop,' he replied. 'I'm not angry. I'm curious as to what's gone on, and I find it interesting and amusing.'

McLaren announced that they would appeal against the stewards' decision to ban them from scoring points in the constructors' championships, while Ron Dennis, with the threat of expulsion still hanging over his head as a result of the Ferrari-gate scandal, now had to deal with this latest controversy. 'Lewis and I were firm with each other,' he admitted when questioned about the heated exchange with his young driver over the radio. 'But going into details serves no function.'

Hamilton made it clear that he wanted answers. 'We sometimes wait a few seconds to make sure we get a clear track,' he said. 'But not if it means delaying your teammate.'

Not surprisingly, Alonso's take on the matter was different. 'We have to wait for the right moment,' he countered. 'That might be five, ten or even forty-five seconds. I was sitting there listening to my engineer count down. It's the same at every race.' Television footage appeared to show that Alonso was looking at Fabrizio Borra, his personal physiotherapist, for a signal, with the man apparently counting down the seconds. 'The team always decides when I get moving,' Alonso added. 'I know it looks odd, because he lost the opportunity to do his lap, but even if I had left five seconds earlier he wouldn't have made it anyway. I think the calculations were wrong. I'm sorry for him, but I leave the pits when told. There have been ten races this season, and that has been going on in nearly all of them.'

Hamilton would not have this at all. 'No, it's not normal,' he responded. 'The lollipop goes up, and the car goes. In the last ten qualifying sessions, the car was sitting there on its own and might have waited a couple of seconds, but not forty.'

British Racing Drivers' Club chairman Damon Hill, an unashamed Hamilton admirer, was an angry observer. 'It seemed like a tactical ploy from Alonso to make sure he was the last person to get a lap in,' said the 1996 world champion. 'You have to say Alonso's basically got what he wanted there. He certainly showed he's not prepared to play a team game if it's at his expense. I think it was a very selfish thing to do, but sometimes selfish guys win.'

Dennis, in another turn of events, said that Hamilton was partly to blame for the confusion. 'We have to wait for the cars to reach operating temperature before we send them down the pit lane ahead of the final part of qualifying,' he explained.

ABOVE: You're not going anywhere! Alonso blocks Hamilton in the pits during final qualifying at the Hungarian Grand Prix.

'It was Fernando's turn to go first and get the benefit of a clear track during the fuel burn off, but Lewis's car was ready earlier. We sent him on his way, but he was supposed to let Fernando by and didn't. That was disappointing.'

Hamilton acknowledged his disobedience. 'If I'd let Alonso through, there was a danger that Kimi Räikkönen might pass me, too,' he said. 'I didn't want to waste an opportunity that had been presented to me. I took a selfish decision but didn't do anything to impede my teammate.'

Incredibly, he insisted that all the ongoing controversy would not deflect his focus from the main job in hand. 'Blanking out the other stuff is a skill I

have learned over the years,' he pointed out. 'I love my job. It is something I have always wanted to do, and I still enjoy it. I always have a smile on my face when I get in the car, so it's easy for me to overcome any problems I have in the team and get on with things in the best way I can.'

This is precisely what he did the following afternoon when he won his third Grand Prix in what was still a remarkably short career and extended his lead in the world drivers' championship. It might have been a largely uneventful race – unlike the pre- and indeed post-race controversies that would rage – but it was undoubtedly Hamilton's best win under the circumstances. He may have been keen to remind people he was still a rookie, but he revealed the killer instincts of a winner in the August heat of central Europe.

PREVIOUS PAGE: Hamilton heads for the first corner in the lead at the Hungaroring.

For once, there was a clean start to the race. Hamilton, in pole, got to the first corner leading, while Kimi Räikkönen, who began the race in third, managed to get past Nick Heidfeld, who had experienced the heady heights of starting second on the grid. During the first lap, however, Alonso found the dirt, which relegated him from sixth to eighth place. By the 16th lap, the race order had remained unchanged as Hamilton built up a lead of 4.5 seconds over Räikkönen. It was sufficient to retain the lead when both he and the Finn went for their first visit to the pits. Although his advantage was then cut to under a second, Hamilton still emerged ahead of Räikkönen when he made his second and final pit stop on lap 50. Again, the Ferrari driver drew to within half a second of the rookie, but Hamilton revealed more of his steely nerve to hold Räikkönen off and win by a margin of 0.7 seconds. Heidfeld grabbed a creditable third ahead of Alonso in fourth, while Felipe Massa, the other increasingly unlikely title challenger, ended up in thirteenth after Ferrari incredibly forgot to refuel his car during qualifying.

Hamilton had just produced a drive not far from perfection. In an example of his thirst for dominance, the first question he asked afterwards was who had set the fastest lap. When he was told it was Räikkönen, the British driver playfully punched the Finn on the arm, before recounting a story that told you everything you needed to know about the mentality of the man. 'This morning I felt a big cloud over my mind because the team weren't getting any points,' he said. 'I didn't know whether everyone hated me, or whether they just hated the situation, or who they were blaming. It was difficult, so I just went into the garage with a smile on my face and tried to remain positive and do everything as normal. I went around the whole team, apologised and we wished each other luck – or most of us did! Then I just got in and did my job, and we won. It just shows the energy we have as a team. And it just proves that nothing can stop us.'

That was how to win favour, although the throwaway comment about 'or most of us did' would become the big story in the aftermath of the race as the full extent of the breakdown in relations between the two McLaren drivers emerged. 'There was only one person I didn't speak to,' Hamilton continued. 'That didn't affect me. Like I said, I just went on

and did my job. Fernando doesn't seem to have been speaking to me since yesterday, so I don't know if that is a problem. If I see him, I will talk to him, but I will not go over and make him feel better.'

It probably would not have helped. Later, Alonso, who now found himself seven points behind Hamilton in the drivers' championship, was visibly seething. His replies to two pertinent questions were terse. First, he was asked whether he would still see out his two-year contract with McLaren. 'I don't know,' he answered. Then, he was asked if he had ever experienced a similar situation in his career. 'Never,' he responded, before launching into a criticism of the stewards' decision to demote him five places on the grid. 'The penalty is not related to any specific rules,' he argued. 'It was a stupid decision, but one of those strange things that happens. The race result was determined by last night's decision. This is like when an unfair penalty kick is called against you in football. You have to keep playing the game with the goal against you.'

Hamilton also shed light on his heated exchange with Dennis, which was an incredible twist, considering their background, in the seemingly never-ending stream of controversies surrounding the McLaren team. 'Ron was not happy,' Hamilton admitted. 'We were professionals, so we sat down and spoke about it. I told him my views. He told me he respected that and that it was part of my personality. We came to a mutual understanding and came to the race with a clean slate. After the argument I had with Ron on the radio, he was angry. I just thought he was teaching me a lesson. I did not think Fernando would do that sort of thing, but I have reasons to believe that this is not the case.'

Dennis, who had just seen fifteen constructors' points lost as a result of Hamilton and Alonso's points not counting because of the qualifying saga, appeared before the world's press with a weary look that revealed the increasing strain of being in charge of two drivers heading for a divorce. 'I don't think either driver is blameless,' he said. 'There is a tremendous amount of pressure on the team, and it comes from two guys who are phenomenally talented and who are leading the championship and looking for every advantage. It's extremely challenging to give both drivers equality, but that is our commitment. If the price of equality is a few bumps or even potholes along the way, I'll take that.'

LEFT: This is getting to be really annoying! Kimi Räikkönen, yet again, cannot find a way past race leader Hamilton.

LEWIS HAMILTON

Unfazed by all the mud flying around, Hamilton left the Hungaroring delighted with his weekend's work. He had managed, once again, to hold off a driver as skilled and as experienced as Kimi Räikkönen, and had extended his lead at the top of the drivers' championship. 'I've had Kimi on my tail a couple of times before, notably in Malaysia, so that helped me today,' he added. 'Today, with some of the problems I had, was one of my hardest races ever. To get points is so important for the championship and for the morale of the team – to show we can beat anyone. There's really no stopping us now.'

RACE RESULT			
	DRIVER	**TEAM**	**POINTS**
1	Lewis Hamilton	McLaren-Mercedes	10
2	Kimi Räikkönen	Ferrari	8
3	Nick Heidfeld	BMW Sauber	6
4	Fernando Alonso	McLaren-Mercedes	5
5	Robert Kubica	BMW Sauber	4
6	Ralf Schumacher	Toyota	3
7	Nico Rosberg	Williams	2
8	Heikki Kovalainen	Renault	1

CONSTRUCTORS' CHAMPIONSHIP AFTER ELEVEN RACES		
	TEAM	**POINTS**
1	McLaren-Mercedes	138
2	Ferrari	119
3	BMW Sauber	71
4	Renault	33
5	Williams	20
6	Red Bull	16
7	Toyota	12
8	Super Aguri	4
9	Honda	1

DRIVERS' CHAMPIONSHIP AFTER ELEVEN RACES		
	DRIVER	**POINTS**
1	Lewis Hamilton	80
2	Fernando Alonso	73
3	Kimi Räikkönen	60
4	Felipe Massa	59
5	Nick Heidfeld	42
6	Robert Kubica	28
7	Giancarlo Fisichella	17
8	Heikki Kovalainen	16
9	Alex Wurz	13
10	Mark Webber	8
10	David Coulthard	8
12	Jarno Trulli	7
12	Nico Rosberg	7
14	Ralf Schumacher	5
15	Takuma Sato	4
16	Jenson Button	1
16	Sebastian Vettel	1

ABOVE: Hamilton congratulates third-placed Nick Heidfeld at the end of the Hungarian Grand Prix.

FACING PAGE: I don't believe it! Hamilton wins again, this time in Hungary.

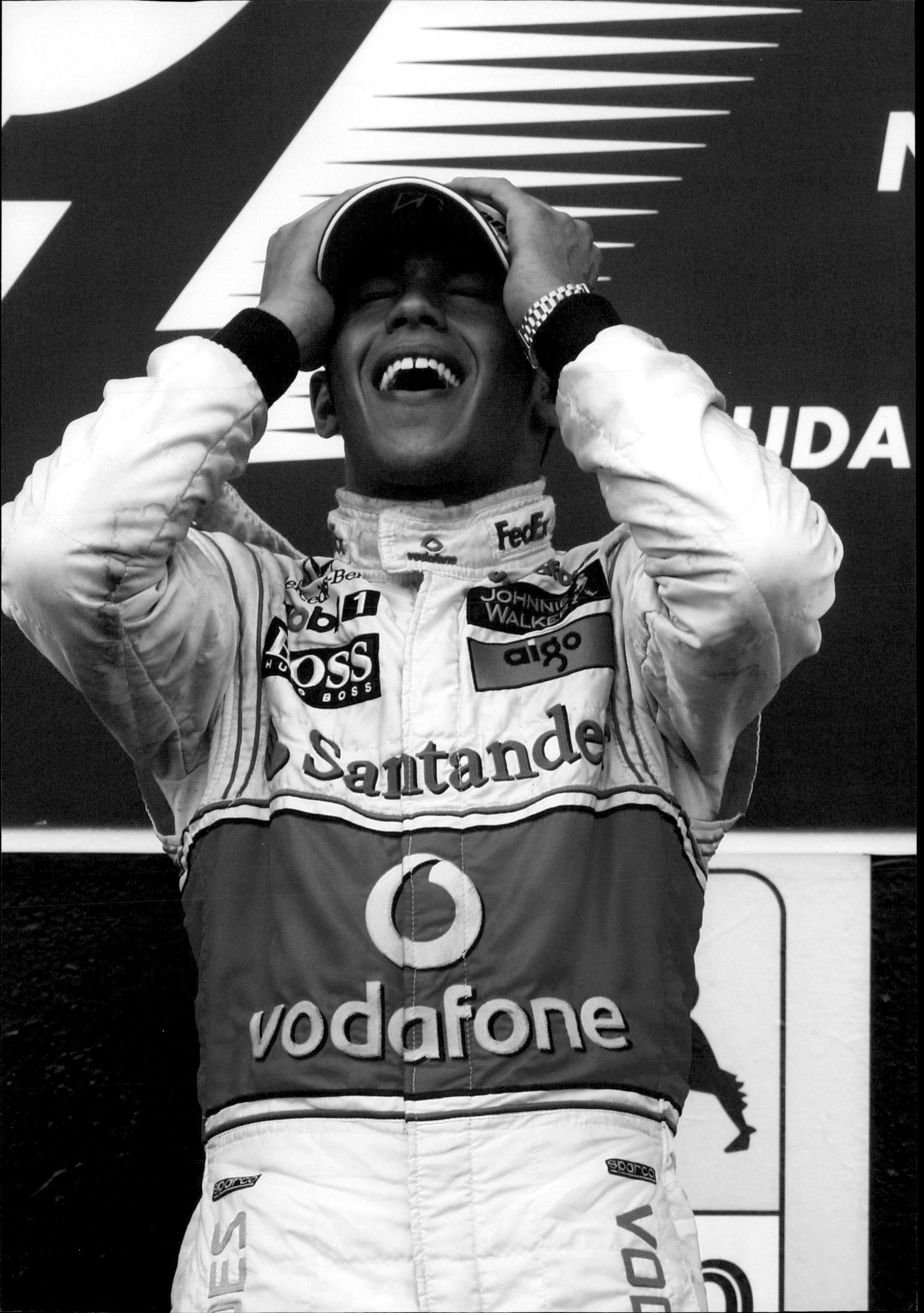
aigo
vodafone

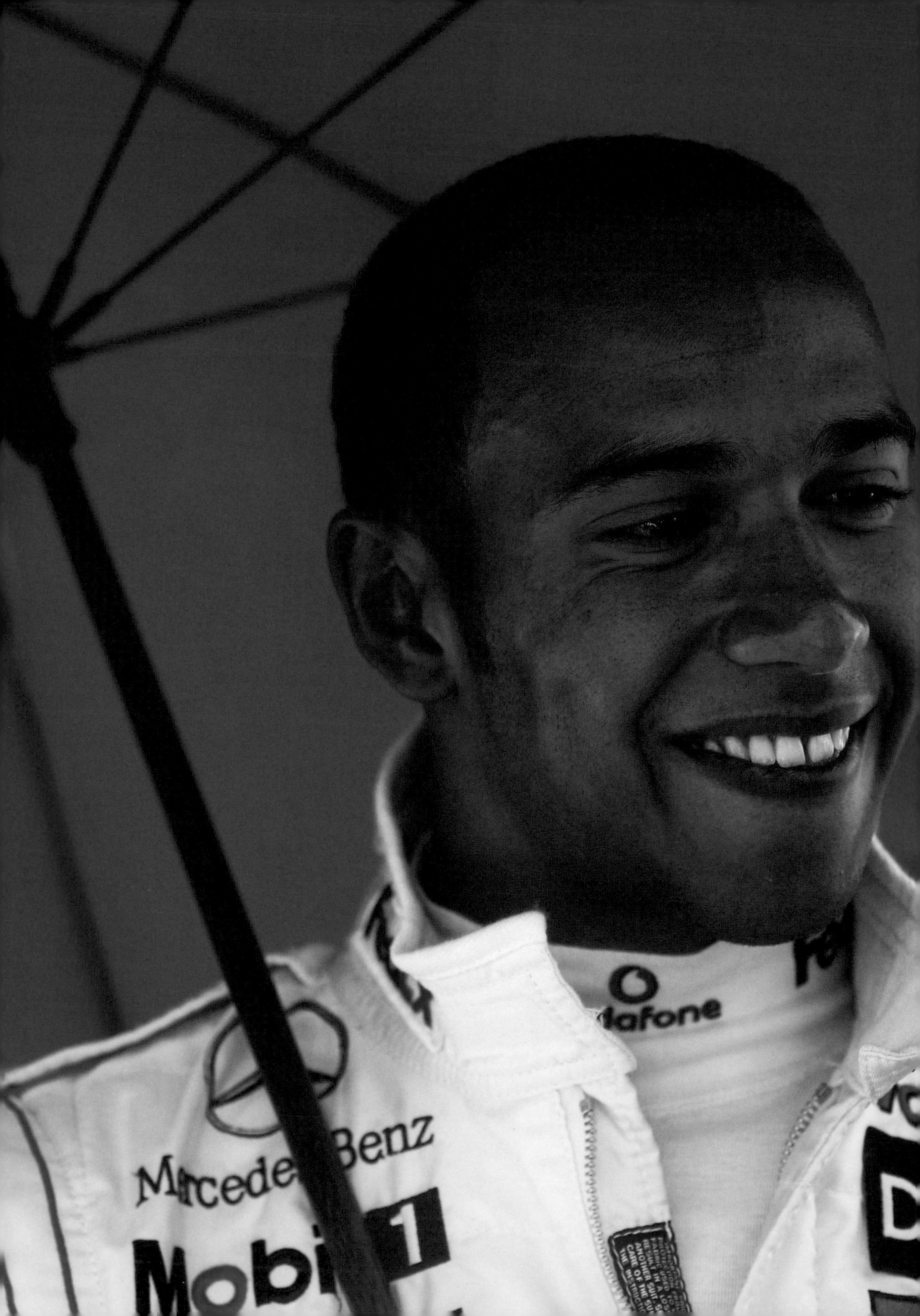
Benz

Race 12

Turkish Grand Prix

Istanbul

Sunday, 26 August 2007

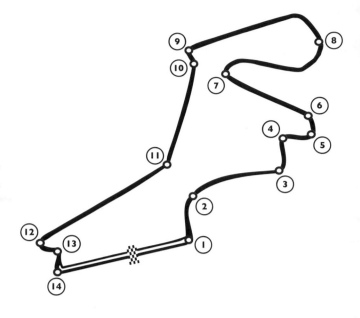

ISTANBUL RACING CIRCUIT

Attendance: 50,000
Weather: sunny, 33 °C
Track temperature: 48 °C
Number of laps: 58
Circuit length: 3.317 miles
Race distance: 192.386 miles
Fastest lap: Kimi Räikkönen, 1:27.295 (lap 57)

Hamilton 5th, 4 points (84)

Ron Dennis believed he had a dream team at his disposal when he named, with justifiable pride, his driver line-up for the 2007 season. A look at the drivers' and constructors' standings prior to the Turkish Grand Prix suggested his selections had been spot on, but with over half of the season completed he had never, in all his experience in Formula One, known a year like it. And if he hoped the furore over what Hamilton had or hadn't done in Hungary – and what Alonso most certainly had in the pit-lane – had subsided, he was gravely mistaken.

Alonso, just seven points adrift of his teammate at the top of the drivers' table, now had the bit between his teeth. A third successive world championship was well within his grasp, and the Spaniard was going to use any method at his disposal to make it become a reality. One such act was to initiate an air of uncertainty over his future whereabouts. 'I don't know,' was his answer to repeated questioning about whether he would be a McLaren driver in 2008. Another ploy was to make reference to Hamilton's actions in Hungary. 'What happened was something new for the team,' he said. 'Hamilton not listening and disobeying them was something they hadn't

experienced, and I guess they wanted to make him see that. I have never heard anything like it. We were first and second in qualifying and nobody was happy. It was one of the most surreal moments I've experienced in Formula One. But anyway, in the next race I guess everything will be back to normal, and we will both try to win.'

The crux of Alonso's problem remained the team mantra that both drivers were, and would continue to be, equal. Dennis, in an uncharacteristic dropping of his guard, expressed his frustrations at the friction that had developed between his drivers. 'When you go through the period of your life between 30 and 60, you often hear the expression "character building", but I can tell you that at 60 years old I don't need my character building any more,' he said, rather resignedly. 'This is extremely challenging for me – emotional and stressful. I'm not alone in having to carry that burden, but, nevertheless, we will continue to function as a Grand Prix team with specific values, and if anybody does not want to be part of those values, irrespective of where they sit in the organisation, ultimately they have a choice.'

He was well aware of the rumours flying around

ABOVE: Alonso had supposedly made up with Hamilton in Istanbul, but it was not long before he was complaining to the world's media again.

the paddock concerning Alonso's future but remained steadfast in his and his team's position. 'It is inevitable that these things are rumoured and discussed in other teams,' he countered. 'We have two drivers who are contracted for several years. We will respect our part of that bargain and that part of the situation. We hope that the drivers respect their part, because that's what a contract is all about.'

Later in the week, Hamilton took a summer's break in St-Tropez on the French Riviera, but he was still keen to clear up some of the mess lingering from the previous race. For a start, he said that he and Alonso would patch up their differences in good time for the Turkish Grand Prix. 'Although we did

not speak on the Sunday of the race, we have spoken a few times since the weekend, and we continue to have a professional working relationship,' Hamilton said. 'In fact, Fernando and I plan to meet up over the holiday period.'

He was also very keen to set the record straight about the allegations that he had used the f-word to Dennis over the car radio. A McLaren statement was issued 'to correct one important matter of untrue, critical commentary'. It continued, 'The team have investigated this claim and reviewed the radio transmissions, and we can categorically confirm that Lewis did not use the f-word at any time during the conversation with the team. The team and Lewis are extremely disappointed that the use of the f-word appears to have been invented and repeated to the media.'

Hamilton, whose image up to this point had been untarnished, was very clear on this matter. 'As an individual in my first year in Formula One, I have done my utmost to conduct myself in a professional and open manner,' he added. 'Of course, I have made mistakes, not least during the last weekend. Those are open to public scrutiny. I have my own regrets and have dealt with the matters arising. However, it is disappointing that inflammatory and untrue material is given to the media and published, which may damage reputations. This inflammatory material is then commented on by others as if it is factual. While I wouldn't normally communicate

through press statements, I felt it important to set this matter straight.'

More problems in the media followed when a series of photographs appeared in the press. Some showed him frolicking with McLaren joint-owner Mansour Ojeh's daughter Sarah in St-Tropez, while others caught him at a West End cinema with another girl. 'I'm not a playboy,' he insisted. 'I'm not dating all these different women. If I was, fair play, write it. But I'm not. I'm trying to lead a normal life.'

He then went into a more detailed explanation of what had actually happened. 'I was supposed to go away with my friends on a lads' holiday. I thought it was a bad idea at the midpoint of the season when I'm leading the world championship. I just needed to

BELOW: From smiles to frowns – Hamilton discovers that being shot at as the leader of the world driver's championship is no fun in Istanbul.

relax, to recover and do some training. I was invited on to Mansour's boat. There was thirteen of us, including the three Ojeh sisters. They all had their boyfriends there. What you don't see in the pictures is the other 12 on the back of the boat also throwing each other in. It wouldn't be so bad if I was getting together with all these women. I'm not. I found out the other day I've slept with Dido. I don't remember it. Now I'm supposed to be dating one of the Ojehs. The other day I went to the cinema with my best friend Mohammed. They said he was my bodyguard and I was seeing this girl, cheating on someone else. It's not me.'

This was not Ron Dennis's major concern, however. He needed, somehow, to stop his drivers from their continual feuding. Hamilton had attempted to meet up with Alonso prior to arriving in Turkey. 'After the last race, I called Fernando and said, "Look, we can't go for the next three weeks without talking or just relying on what the media is saying – that we are at war,"' Hamilton explained. 'So I said we needed to meet and discuss the last race and how we could move forward, because at the end of the day we are teammates and need to get on.'

With holiday commitments on both sides, this get-together finally took place in Turkey. A meeting was set up two days before qualifying in a downtown hotel in central Istanbul, forty minutes from the circuit at Istanbul Park, across the Bosporus on the Asian side of the city. Martin Whitmarsh, Norbert Haug, Hamilton and Alonso were all present. After some small talk, they got down to the nitty-gritty. 'I put my hands up and apologised for everything that went on in the last race,' Hamilton later revealed. 'And he said, "Me, too. I have nothing against you. It may have seemed it was aimed at you, but we need to figure out how to move forward."'

Alonso backed this story up. 'Everything is OK now, and the past is the past,' the Spaniard promised. 'I talked with Lewis, and we had to laugh. We tried to understand why everyone's trying to put us in a fight. It is not the truth.'

Not even Hamilton could push himself to promise that the issue was completely dead. 'I'm not saying that all of a sudden everything is bright, but we've come back and all settled our differences and where we want to go,' he said. 'I feel very comfortable and confident that we both have the opportunity to go out and battle each other. That's what racing is all about.

I have no doubt that I have a great opportunity to win the championship. I'm in the best spot, I've got a great team and a great car, and I'm very competitive. As long as I don't make any mistakes, I don't see why I can't win it.'

Bernie Ecclestone, as always, was in town, and he was delighted with the way interest in the sport had been reignited by the emergence of Hamilton and the dogfight on the circuit between him and Alonso. He reckoned the Spaniard would eventually come out on top as world champion, but he could not praise Hamilton's achievements enough. 'I suppose you would have to say Alonso is the favourite because of his experience, but the way the other guy [Hamilton] is performing if you took his hat off and put bloody Schumacher's hat on, you'd say Schumacher was driving, wouldn't you?' he said, in typical 'Bernie-speak'. He also argued that the tension between the two would dissipate if it became obvious that one of them could not win the world title. 'If one gets into a position where the other one can't really catch him and he needs a bit of help, maybe that's what will happen,' he reasoned. 'If you and I are in the same team against each other, as long as we are still competing we are probably going to be a little bit edgy with each other. But I think when you are obviously clear in front and I can't do anything about it, then I will want to help you. So that's when you'll see the test.'

Never satisfied, Ecclestone's only regret was that the tussle for the drivers' title was not between four drivers, with Ferrari looking increasingly unlikely to be involved at the end of the season. 'I'd like to see both the McLaren cars stop and Ferrari get some points and have four runners in contention,' Ecclestone explained. 'You'd have to put your money on McLaren, but you never know.'

Saturday's qualifying session was surrounded in more controversy when it emerged that Alonso had revealed to a Spanish radio station that his take on events was actually rather different to what he had previously stated. With his and Hamilton's hands still warm from their handshake 48 hours earlier, Alonso reiterated his displeasure at the team's insistence on treating both the current world champion and his heir apparent equally. 'We're not the best of friends,'

FACING PAGE: The boss tells it how it is – Bernie Ecclestone in conversation with Ferrari's Kimi Räikkönen at Istanbul Park.

RIGHT: Ferrari's Felipe Massa leads virtually from start to finish in Turkey.

he said, referring to Hamilton. 'But we respect each other, and I don't have a problem with him. If I do have a problem, it's with the team. My belief is that last year McLaren were nowhere. I remember how the car was going when we tested it in December and how it went in the Australian Grand Prix. I have brought the expertise of a double world champion to the team, and the car is now six-tenths of a second quicker per lap. This has not been reflected at any time when we two drivers have been competing against each other. That's basically the quarrel I have had for the whole season.'

His mood would not have brightened after he finished Saturday's qualification in fourth place on the grid, two behind Hamilton and three behind Felipe Massa on pole. Hamilton was understandably much happier with his day's work. 'It's positive for me to be two spots ahead of Fernando, and now I must try and get as many points today and finish ahead of him,' he said with regard to the qualifying result. 'I'm confident we'll have a good race.'

After the race, a beleaguered Ron Dennis had to deal with Alonso's latest outburst. 'Fernando is focusing on one piece of data,' he said, referring to the six-tenths improvement that Alonso was suggesting was down to him. 'It's been taken out of context in light of other pieces of data that have all helped to improve our performance, such as a change of tyres.'

That night, Hamilton expanded on the invasion of his privacy by the media, a subject that was still bothering him, despite his outburst earlier in the week. He felt so intimidated by the intrusion that he admitted he would most probably move abroad to escape the spotlight. 'I'm definitely contemplating living outside the UK,' he announced. 'I've always dreamed of living in London. I'd still do anything to have my own apartment there, but it will become more and more difficult. Every time I go to London, cameras appear from God knows where. Pressure on the track doesn't get to me. I'm able to manage it. But in your personal life, it affects you. This year has been a complete roller coaster for me, and it looks like I'm doing things perfectly, but I make mistakes like anyone. I can be walking along the street and people look at me very differently. All they do is read what's in the papers and all the crap that's put out. You have to brush it off, but some can do that better than others.'

Ironically, Hamilton had some sympathy for his teammate on this subject. 'I can see from the experience of Fernando what can happen,' he explained. 'He's so big in Spain, he can't stay there because he can't go anywhere and live a normal life. I thought that wouldn't be the case in the UK. When I was working my way up to Formula One, I was only thinking about getting a drive for a great team and racing. I didn't think about the pros and cons, about the fact that you

will pick up sponsors or that people will notice you more. It's all new, and I'm trying to get used to it. My whole holiday was in the papers. I was trying to relax, but I couldn't swim because the cameras were waiting to get 10,000 euros for the pictures.

'It's not such an issue when people come up to me. I get a buzz out of one or two people coming up now and then. When I came out of the cinema, I didn't get crowded by people, but I got almost bullied by photographers because they wanted pictures. Things like that make me not want to be in the UK.'

Whatever his gripes were, Hamilton remained his ultra-professional self at Istanbul Park. The year before, he had produced one of the drives of the season in GP2 when he recovered from sixteenth to finish second. On the Saturday, he made a point of watching the 2007 GP2 series race at the circuit, all in the cause of research. 'I wanted to see how

the guys on the dirtier side of the track coped at the start,' he admitted. 'That's something I'll have to deal with.' He had also been preparing for turn eight, a notorious and super-quick left-hander, through which drivers are exposed to 4.5 g of lateral force for many seconds. 'It feels different to how I remember it in GP2 when I had no power-steering.

The steering may be lighter now, but you're going through there much more quickly, so there's a lot more of a load on your neck. It's a great corner, but it will be hard work over 58 laps.'

And hard work it proved to be. Hamilton was undone by a slice of misfortune that benefited Alonso, although it could have been so much worse

LEFT: Torn to shreds – Hamilton's tyre bursts at Istanbul Park, but he still steers his car to a fifth-place finish.

From then on, it was Ferrari's show, with Massa and Räikkönen battling it out to see who would take the top place on the podium. The Brazilian, with the advantage of pole, won the day, with the Finn coming in second, but the real drama of the race unfolded behind them. With 15 laps remaining, and with Hamilton holding down a comfortable third place, his front-right tyre blew when he was travelling at 190 mph. This, as any driver will testify, is a highly dangerous occurrence, and Hamilton needed all his wits to stay on the track. The incident happened midway round the 3.3-mile circuit, which meant the MP4–22 then had to limp its way round the remainder of the track with a flapping tyre, before emergency work could take place in the pits to replace it. A grateful Alonso shot past Hamilton at this point, as did Nick Heidfeld, and the young McLaren driver had to make do with a disappointing fifth. And Alonso's third place meant that Hamilton's lead at the top of the drivers' table had been cut from seven to five points.

'I didn't have any warning,' a frustrated Hamilton said afterwards. 'I exited the fast left-hander at turn eight and saw some bits fly off the tyre. As soon as I hit the brakes at turn nine, the tyre exploded. The wheel locked up, and the car was moving around, and I was just going straight. I was very, very lucky to get the car stopped and turned. I thought I wouldn't get back to the pits. As soon as the tyre went, I braked and nothing was really happening. It looked like I was going to go through the gravel and into the wall. The tyre was getting worse and worse. When I got to turn 12, the car wouldn't steer. I got to the pit lane and nearly went into the wall. It was a real fight, and I'm glad I got it there. The front wing was damaged, and I was worried it was going to damage some other bits on the car. I just saw my competitors going past.'

Despite this, he remained, as usual, both philosophical and upbeat. 'It depends how you look at the glass: half-full or half-empty. I don't count myself lucky. I think it was unlucky that the tyre went. I was the only one with a shredded tyre. It's racing, but I'm still confident for the rest of the season. There are still five races to go, and I'm still five points clear. I lost four points today, but I'll figure out a way to get them back somewhere else.

for the rookie. The start was not perfect from the British driver's perspective. Kimi Räikkönen, who began in third place on the grid, managed to nudge ahead of Hamilton into second place. Behind them, Robert Kubica and Nick Heidfeld were both able to jump ahead of Alonso, dropping the Spaniard down to sixth.

ABOVE: Guys, we've got a problem – in the pits during the Turkish Grand Prix, Hamilton requires a new tyre and fast.

LEWIS HAMILTON

On the in-lap, I was thinking that it would be great if I went to the next race and got five more points than anyone else.'

Alonso only finished third in what was his hundredth Grand Prix, but he still left Turkey happy. 'I won't remember this Grand Prix for the rest of my life, but it's the best news I could get out of this weekend,' he announced as he left Istanbul Park and started making plans for Monza. 'The better one, the luckier one, will win the title.' With the Italian Grand Prix two weeks away, both Hamilton and Alonso would have wondered which of them was the better and, more importantly, which the luckier of the two.

RACE RESULT			
	DRIVER	TEAM	POINTS
1	Felipe Massa	Ferrari	10
2	Kimi Räikkönen	Ferrari	8
3	Fernando Alonso	McLaren-Mercedes	6
4	Nick Heidfeld	BMW Sauber	5
5	Lewis Hamilton	McLaren-Mercedes	4
6	Heikki Kovalainen	Renault	3
7	Nico Rosberg	Williams	2
8	Robert Kubica	BMW Sauber	1

CONSTRUCTORS' CHAMPIONSHIP AFTER TWELVE RACES		
	TEAM	POINTS
1	McLaren-Mercedes	148
2	Ferrari	137
3	BMW Sauber	77
4	Renault	36
5	Williams	22
6	Red Bull	16
7	Toyota	12
8	Super Aguri	4
9	Honda	1

DRIVERS' CHAMPIONSHIP AFTER TWELVE RACES		
	DRIVER	POINTS
1	Lewis Hamilton	84
2	Fernando Alonso	79
3	Felipe Massa	69
4	Kimi Räikkönen	68
5	Nick Heidfeld	47
6	Robert Kubica	29
7	Heikki Kovalainen	19
8	Giancarlo Fisichella	17
9	Alex Wurz	13
10	Nico Rosberg	9
11	Mark Webber	8
11	David Coulthard	8
13	Jarno Trulli	7
14	Ralf Schumacher	5
15	Takuma Sato	4
16	Jenson Button	1
16	Sebastian Vettel	1

ABOVE: It's Ferrari's day in Turkey, but Alonso begins to haul back Hamilton's lead.

Race 13

Italian Grand Prix

Monza

Sunday, 9 September 2007

Attendance: 90,000
Weather: sunny, 25 °C
Track temperature: 35 °C
Number of laps: 53
Circuit length: 3.6 miles
Race distance: 190.8 miles
Fastest lap: Fernando Alonso, 1:22.871 (lap 15)

Hamilton 2nd, 8 points (92)

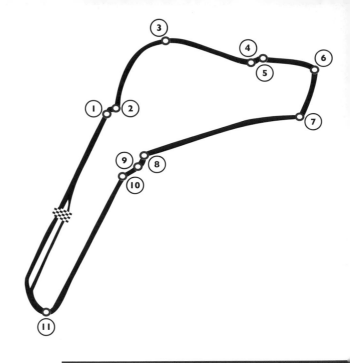

AUTODROMO NAZIONALE MONZA

Nobody truly believed the scandal that had engulfed Formula One had gone away for good, and in the run-up to the Italian Grand Prix it reared its head again, only this time with far more serious connotations. New evidence emerged in the Ferrari espionage affair, and as a result the FIA scrapped the appeal hearing scheduled for Paris the following week, instead calling a meeting of the World Motor Sport Council to hear the case. It was with this new threat to McLaren's dominance in both the drivers' and constructors' championships that Hamilton, Alonso, Dennis and company arrived in Monza for the home Grand Prix of a resurgent Ferrari.

On the day of their arrival in Italy, the spy plot thickened. It emerged that Alonso was the alleged recipient of an unsolicited email containing information about the Ferrari car. The message was supposedly posted in his inbox by McLaren test driver Pedro de la Rosa, who in turn had received the mail from Mike Coughlan, the McLaren chief designer, who was at the centre of the whole affair, together with Ferrari's Nigel Stepney. Requested by the FIA to disclose what he knew, the world champion had little

option but to comply. De la Rosa and Hamilton were also contacted by the FIA, although there was no suggestion that Hamilton was caught up in the mess.

Indeed, it prompted Hamilton to deliver an impassioned defence of his team and a pledge to deliver the goods at the home of Ferrari. 'Victory at Monza would definitely lift spirits,' said the rookie. 'That's why we've pushed so hard to make sure we come here strong. Beating Ferrari on their home ground would be a huge blow to their whole team. That will make us extremely happy. It would be a great feeling to do that because of what they are putting our team through. I know the people here, and I think we are being treated unfairly. So, to come here and to do our talking on the track, that's what we'll try and do. That is absolutely the best way to do it.'

The next day at the first free practice session, the FIA released the contents of a letter that it had sent to all three McLaren drivers, which requested they hand over any material in their possession that contained confidential technical information from Ferrari. Written by FIA president Max Mosley, it stated, 'You will appreciate that there is a duty on all competitors and super licence holders to ensure the fairness and legitimacy of the Formula One world championship. It is therefore imperative that if you do have such information, you make it available to us without delay.' He went on to say that although the drivers were not threatened with sanctions themselves, they faced 'serious consequences' if they failed to hand over incriminating material.

You would think all this might have had some kind of negative effect on the McLaren drivers, but in the second session of free practice Alonso and Hamilton were the quickest and second-quickest drivers. 'As soon as the cars start and you are doing some laps, then you don't think about any problems,' Alonso insisted.

Hamilton continued to impress fascinated observers with his cool demeanour as the storm clouds continued to form. 'I wouldn't say mental focus is an easy thing,' he said. 'It is just something that I've built up over the years. I've learned from my dad and those small experiences that you have. It could be playing golf or playing PlayStation with my brother. If you are getting beaten at something, you learn to control yourself and rise above it and come back stronger. That has always been something my dad has forced upon me, so I think with his help I have grown to be quite strong. It is going to be extremely tough, as it has all year, but the key for me is to try and fine-tune all the rough edges. The world title is very much on.'

Hamilton backed up this defiant message the following day at qualifying when he managed to haul himself up into second place on the grid for the Italian Grand Prix. Alonso, his teammate and nearest challenger for the world title, pipped him to pole, but the afternoon told us everything we needed to know: whatever accusations were being levelled at McLaren, they were still on top of their game. This was some achievement, especially as it later emerged that the Italian *carabinieri* had served five writs on McLaren team employees, including team boss Ron Dennis. He had already vowed to clear his name at the World Motor Sports Council hearing in Paris, which was taking place the following Thursday, but now it seemed he would have to defend himself in an Italian court as well. Nigel Stepney and Mike Coughlan also received writs. Italian police sources let it be known that hundreds of telephone calls and text messages had been traced between Stepney and Coughlan, which contradicted Coughlan's earlier claim that his contact with the former Ferrari employee had been 'minimal'.

Once again, Hamilton, who was pleased to have come second in qualifying but disappointed to be pressed on the fast-moving espionage story, was required to defend his colleagues. 'This has been a big knock for the team,' he said. 'But I have worked with these guys for many years, and I have no doubts, nothing has gone on.'

In Dennis's opinion, this was further confirmation that the sport was waging a vendetta against his team. 'There are a few people round here who would like me to retire,' he responded. 'If that proved to be in the interests of the company, then I wouldn't hesitate to do it. But we think we are leading the championship fair and square.'

With rumours, accusations and counter-accusations rife in the paddock, the FIA felt it necessary to issue a denial that they were pursuing a feud against McLaren. 'The suggestion that the FIA's ongoing investigation is about anything other than the pursuit of sporting fairness demonstrates a blinding refusal to accept basic facts,' it said.

It had got to the point that the racing was almost being overlooked. Further rumours that Dennis was considering withdrawing both his drivers and his team from the world championships if they received a draconian punishment following the World Motor Sports Council meeting started to be aired, and with back-to-back Grands Prix at Monza and Spa in Belgium within a week of each other Bernie Ecclestone was keen to have his say. 'People come to me and say Ron is going to withdraw,' he said. 'I've no idea what he's going to do. But if they've done something wrong and they've got a big advantage, you've got to take it on the chin and say, "I've been caught with my hand in the till. Let's see how we can get out of it." If I'd been in that position, I wouldn't withdraw. I'd try to straighten it out. If you let someone get away with that, what's next? Then there are no rules and regulations. It's make your own rules time.'

Still, the most influential figure in the sport did have some kind words to say about Hamilton. 'I would love to see Lewis win the world championship,' he added. 'I think everyone would. Schumacher's gone, and now we've got this new guy who's wonderful. He's as good as Michael, certainly on the track.'

FACING PAGE: The *tifosi* let their feelings be known – McLaren receive no sympathy for their part in the espionage scandal at Monza.

With Felipe Massa in third place after qualifying, in front of Nick Heidfeld and Kimi Räikkönen, who was back down in fifth, it was a perfect opportunity for McLaren to show their worth where it mattered most and in front of the fiercely partisan *tifosi*. And this is exactly what they went on to do in emphatic style after a clean start from Alonso and a brave effort from Hamilton, who still managed to reach the first corner in second place, despite being swamped by both Ferraris when Räikkönen jumped past Heidfeld at the start. Once again, the safety car was employed early on when David Coulthard's Red Bull hit Giancarlo Fisichella's Renault at the first chicane on the second lap and crashed at the 'Curva Grande'. The race only restarted on lap seven, when Alonso held off Hamilton's challenge to take the lead into turn one.

Matters got worse for Ferrari when Massa's stop–start season continued. He dived into the pits on the ninth lap to have a handling problem checked, only to retire shortly afterwards. With both Alonso and Hamilton making their first pit stops, Räikkönen took over the lead on lap 20, much to the delight of the *tifosi*, but this was as good as it got. Five laps later, he too diverted into the pits, and when he re-emerged he found himself back behind the two McLaren drivers. On lap forty, the Finn was promoted to second place behind Alonso after Hamilton pitted again, but the young rookie passed the sole remaining Ferrari driver three laps later at turn one, and the top three remained in place for the final laps of the race. Alonso took the chequered flag by six seconds from Hamilton, with Räikkönen a disappointing third on Ferrari home ground and the BMW Saubers of Heidfeld and Kubica fourth and fifth respectively.

With only one Grand Prix in Italy in 2007 – the San Marino race had been shelved because of the poor state of the circuit at Imola – it was ironic that this turned out to be McLaren's first-ever one–two at the iconic home of Ferrari in forty-one years of trying. The sight of the Italian minister of justice handing out the trophies on the podium after the race only added to the irony. It was all too much for Ron Dennis, who was understandably emotional after what he had experienced over the previous few

RIGHT: Hamilton flashes past the *tifosi* during qualifying for the Italian Grand Prix.

days, and he openly wept in the arms of his wife Lisa. 'We said on the track what we had to say,' he said moments later. 'It's been challenging. I was considering well before this matter that this would be the year in which I would stop attending Grands Prix. In these circumstances, I don't want to feel I'm being pushed into something that's not part of the agenda.'

He had already instructed his company to release a statement with regard to the latest developments that had dominated the weekend at Monza. 'We did receive some contact from the Italian authorities on Saturday, but we were not charged with anything,' it confirmed. 'We strongly suspect that the nature and timing of this wholly unnecessary contact, just before the start of qualifying, was to disrupt our preparation for this important session and Thursday's hearing. McLaren is completely confident that were any proceedings of this type ever to be brought we would be completely exonerated.'

Just about the only McLaren employee looking completely happy with his weekend's work was Fernando Alonso. The double world champion had dominated at Monza, claiming the holy trinity of pole position, fastest lap and race win, and in doing so he had reduced Hamilton's lead at the top of the drivers' table to just three points. 'It was the perfect weekend for me,' the satisfied Spaniard announced afterwards, which sounded a little strange bearing in mind the huge shadow cast over his team. 'Sometimes everything seems to go in the right direction. Sometimes I have started well here in Monza, but I always then had some problems in the race to make me miss the victory, so to win here for the first time is very special. Now I have to keep the momentum going. I will approach Spa focused to win next week. That is the goal. Nothing really changes with this win. I arrived here focused. I wanted to win the last five races. Four are left. I will go for it.'

Hamilton, after a mixed afternoon, was a little more aware of the bigger picture. 'It would be great for us to win the drivers' and constructors' titles to show that even with these problems nothing can bring us down,' he said. 'We're unstoppable.' However, he did admit to thinking about the worst-case scenario come Thursday's World Motor Sport Council meeting. 'If you sit down and think about it, I could have what I've worked for, and what all the team has worked for, taken away from me next week. And

when you really think about it, you think, "Wow, I could be out of a job next weekend." And then what happens? It was going so well, and then you just get this big knife that cuts off your blood line. It is a bit disappointing when you read things about it – I won't go into it because I'll get emotional – but I really do have such a great belief in my team. I have 100 per

cent confidence in them, so that's why it's easy to stay relaxed. To be honest, it's not something I need to focus on. I am leading the world championship, and I need to focus on my job. I never actually thought I'd be sitting here saying I hate something about Formula One. But there are people wanting to be bigger than the others. That's just incredible. I would say to you

all that Ron has always been very, very loyal to me, has always given me the opportunity to succeed and he has always been such a great man to me.'

It was this desire to stick by his team that had driven Hamilton on when he had bounced back on lap 40 to

BELOW: The heat is on! Anthony Hamilton shields his son on the grid before the start of the Italian Grand Prix.

PREVIOUS PAGE: Taking a short cut – Hamilton is forced to cut corners at turn two at Monza.

overtake Räikkönen and claim second place. 'I came out of the pits right behind Kimi, and I knew that I had two laps maximum to get the best out of my new soft-compound tyres before they went off slightly. The tyres felt great, and the car felt great as well. I wanted to stick it down the inside of the Ferrari. I wanted to do it for the team, as I wanted to let them know how much they'd worked for it. So, I ran two laps really as fast as I could go, launched myself down the inside going into the first corner and managed to pull it off. It was a nice moment in a weekend that's not all been nice.' This momentary downer was soon replaced by the reality of his situation in the race for the world title. 'The last two races, Fernando has finished ahead of me,' Hamilton continued. 'But if you had said at the start of the season that I would be in this position, I'd have said, "Get out of here." So, we fight on.'

McLaren also received support from their oldest rival. Sir Frank Williams and Dennis had vied for the world championships for many years, and both had been hugely successful, usually at each other's expense. However, on this issue, Williams felt that too much was being made of what was actually a regular occurrence in the sport. 'It seems that McLaren and Ron are in a bit of trouble with the FIA,' Williams said. 'The thing to keep in mind, though, is that every time we take an employee from BMW, or we lose one to Honda, or a Renault man goes to so and so, there's always some transfer of information.'

Later that same night, Dennis finally sat down with Italian court representatives, who waited patiently until a McLaren lawyer could be summoned. 'The gentlemen were extremely polite and discreet,' the McLaren boss admitted. 'We were not accused of anything. We were not charged with anything. They were not aggressive and were understanding that I had other responsibilities on the day. The meeting simply established which McLaren executives would need representation if called to attend any hearing in Italy. It was perhaps unfortunate that this meeting took place at the circuit, but they were not in any way hostile. Their behaviour was impeccable, and I understood completely that they were seeking to follow a process laid down under Italian law.'

ABOVE: Somebody loves him – Hamilton fans know how to spell at Monza, even if they are surrounded by Ferrari supporters.

LEWIS HAMILTON

His words were measured and his demeanour restrained. Despite creating McLaren history that day in Monza, it was not really the time for celebration. 'We always wanted to win, and to have McLaren's first one–two at Monza is special,' Dennis concluded. 'I have tried to maintain a disciplined approach to the weekend and stay focused on the important issues. We now have to address the next hurdle, as it were. It has not been easy. The entire team has done a fantastic job on and off the track in difficult circumstances.' These circumstances were about to become even more difficult.

RACE RESULT			
	DRIVER	**TEAM**	**POINTS**
1	Fernando Alonso	McLaren-Mercedes	10
2	Lewis Hamilton	McLaren-Mercedes	8
3	Kimi Räikkönen	Ferrari	6
4	Nick Heidfeld	BMW Sauber	5
5	Robert Kubica	BMW Sauber	4
6	Nico Rosberg	Williams	3
7	Heikki Kovalainen	Renault	2
8	Jenson Button	Honda	1

CONSTRUCTORS' CHAMPIONSHIP AFTER THIRTEEN RACES		
	TEAM	**POINTS**
1	McLaren-Mercedes	166
2	Ferrari	143
3	BMW Sauber	86
4	Renault	38
5	Williams	25
6	Red Bull	16
7	Toyota	12
8	Super Aguri	4
9	Honda	2

ABOVE: Hamilton congratulates Alonso in *parc fermé* for winning the Italian Grand Prix.

FACING PAGE: Another win, another trophy – McLaren boss Ron Dennis takes the spoils once again, but his joy is short-lived.

DRIVERS' CHAMPIONSHIP AFTER THIRTEEN RACES		
	DRIVER	**POINTS**
1	Lewis Hamilton	92
2	Fernando Alonso	89
3	Kimi Räikkönen	74
4	Felipe Massa	69
5	Nick Heidfeld	52
6	Robert Kubica	33
7	Heikki Kovalainen	21
8	Giancarlo Fisichella	17
9	Alex Wurz	13
10	Nico Rosberg	12
11	Mark Webber	8
11	David Coulthard	8
13	Jarno Trulli	7
14	Ralf Schumacher	5
15	Takuma Sato	4
16	Jenson Button	2
17	Sebastian Vettel	1

Race 14

Belgian Grand Prix

Spa

Sunday, 16 September 2007

Attendance: 165,000 for the complete race weekend
Weather: sunny, 22 °C
Track temperature: 37 °C
Number of laps: 44
Circuit length: 4.352 miles
Race distance: 191.488 miles
Fastest lap: Felipe Massa, 1:48.036 (lap 34)

Hamilton 4th, 5 points (97)

CIRCUIT DE SPA-FRANCORCHAMPS

The espionage scandal had ravaged Formula One all summer, and by the time the relevant parties pitched up in Paris to attend the World Motor Sports Council hearing everyone involved just wanted an end to the matter. With only four races remaining in 2007, the drivers had managed to make it one of the most memorable seasons for the past decade, and four still had a chance to be crowned world champion. The sooner everyone could get back to concentrating on the racing, the better, especially after the atmosphere in Monza had been contaminated with poisonous chatter.

Before Lewis Hamilton could start dealing with the challenges the famous old circuit deep in the Ardennes would throw at him, he first had to attend the hearing in person after being called as a shock witness. As it turned out, even though he was one of the 19-man contingent from McLaren, Hamilton did not make any contribution.

For the second time in seven weeks, the sport's highest authority would decide whether any penalties should be meted out. Given the reconvening of the 26-man panel, the signs were ominous, suggesting that the new evidence was serious and could result in a severe punishment.

Speaking at the Frankfurt Motor Show, Luca di Montezemolo, Ferrari's president, spoke for everyone involved in the sport. 'It's in our interests that this ugly story ends quickly and most of all it ends with the truth,' he said. It was a sentiment few could disagree with.

The Thursday before the Belgian Grand Prix proved to be momentous. After a ten-hour meeting in the French capital, the FIA's council concluded that leaked details of Ferrari's 2007 car had been used by McLaren to gain a competitive advantage. The good news was that McLaren's drivers were exonerated and escaped a points deduction that would have destroyed Hamilton's dreams of becoming the first-ever rookie world champion. The bad news, however, was that McLaren was hit with a record-breaking $100-million fine and stripped of all their points in the constructors' championship after being found guilty of cheating. In addition, the team were told that they faced further sanctions if their car for the following year was found to have benefited from any of the secret Ferrari data.

An ashen Ron Dennis attempted to put a brave face on the events when he emerged into the Paris night.

ABOVE: Hamilton arrives at the World Motor Sport Council's hearing in Paris, unsure whether his season will be scuppered by the espionage scandal.

'The most important thing is that we will be going racing this weekend, the rest of the season and every season,' he responded. 'This means that our drivers can continue to compete for the world championship. However, having been at the hearing today, I do not accept that we deserve to be penalised in this way. Today's evidence given to the FIA by our drivers, engineers and staff clearly demonstrated that we did not use leaked information to gain a competitive advantage. We have the best drivers and the best car, and we intend to win the championship.'

A hearing in December would determine whether McLaren would be hit by any further penalties, but Dennis remained defiant. 'There will be no issue for the 2008 season, as we have not at any stage used the intellectual property of any other team,' he insisted. The FIA's verdict handed Ferrari the constructors' title on a plate, with nearest challengers BMW Sauber, who moved up from third to second as a result of the World Motor Sport Council's findings, too far behind. Predictably, Ferrari welcomed the news. 'In light of new evidence, facts and behaviour of an extremely serious nature and grossly prejudicial to the interest of the sport have been further demonstrated. Ferrari is satisfied that the truth has now emerged.'

This made the previous record fines pale into insignificance. In 2006, the organisers of the Turkish Grand Prix were fined $2.5 million for allowing the Turkish Cypriot leader to present the winner's prize. In 2002, Ferrari and drivers Michael Schumacher and Rubens Barrichello were fined $1 million at the Austrian Grand Prix when Barrichello, who dominated the race, was ordered to let Schumacher win. Half the fine was suspended for a year. And in 1998, the Hungarian Grand Prix organisers were fined $1 million after a track invasion.

The sport's reaction to this stunning news was instant. 'I'm absolutely staggered,' said Sir Stirling Moss. 'This is terrible. The whole of motor racing has been shaken. The only thing the World Motor Sport Council has done right is to allow the drivers to keep their points. Ron Dennis is not an easy man, but I feel he's been done down. I really do not believe he would have known about it [Coughlan's possession of the Ferrari data]. OK, he's the captain of the ship, but I would put a lot of my money on his integrity.'

Sir Jackie Stewart was another Formula One legend who had his say. 'Even if they were found guilty of the crime, it does not justify this type of penalty,' he stated.

Dennis, despite the damage to his integrity, was not prepared to let it lie. 'Much has been made of emails and text messages to and from our drivers,' he continued. 'The World Motor Sport Council received statements from Fernando Alonso, Lewis Hamilton and Pedro de la Rosa stating categorically that no Ferrari information had been used by McLaren and that they had not passed any confidential data to the team. The entire engineering team – in excess of 140 people – provided statements to the FIA affirming that they had never received or used the Ferrari information. We have never denied that the information from Ferrari was in the personal possession of one of our employees. The issue is: was the information used by McLaren? This is not the case, and it has not been proven today.'

The council did not quite see it that way, hence the record fine and exclusion from the constructors' championship, but Dennis remained defiant. 'We are continually asked: if McLaren didn't use the information, what was the reason for Stepney and Coughlan collecting all this data about Ferrari? We can only speculate, as neither Coughlan nor Stepney gave evidence today, but we do know that they were both seeking employment with other teams, as already confirmed by Honda and Toyota.'

At least the drivers could carry on relatively unaffected by the FIA's draconian measures. 'Due to the exceptional circumstances, in which the FIA gave the team's drivers immunity from punishment in return for providing evidence, there is no penalty in regard to drivers' points,' the FIA confirmed in a statement.

BELOW: Legal eagles – McLaren boss Ron Dennis comes to Paris fully armed with representatives but is still thrown out of the constructors' championship.

Despite the severity of the fine, it was an indication of the size of McLaren and success enjoyed by Dennis that this was far from a crippling setback. The monies would be paid partly as a fine and partly in returned prize funds. 'We have a turnover of $450 million to $500 million a year, and we are debt free,' explained Dennis. 'This is a very strong company.' He also insisted that there was no chance of him resigning. 'I'm committed to this company, and I'm very passionate about motor racing,' he added.

People might have hoped for a fresh start at free practice the following day, but the fallout from the World Motor Sport Council hearing continued when the true extent of Alonso's declining relationship with McLaren came to the fore. It was not just with his teammate that the double world champion had problems. His increasing anger and frustration at his team's refusal to treat him as their premier asset had resulted in a total breakdown between him and his boss during the Hungarian Grand Prix.

It was reported that on the morning of the race, and with Alonso still smarting from being put back five places on the grid after blocking teammate Hamilton, the Spaniard had confronted Dennis, allegedly asking to be released from his contract and also telling the McLaren boss that he had information that could lead to the team being thrown out of the championship. Dennis had reacted in the only way he could. He had picked up the telephone and called Max Mosley. 'I want to stress that once I became aware that new evidence might exist, which I did on the morning of the Hungarian Grand Prix, I immediately phoned the FIA to keep them informed.'

It was probably just as well. The FIA released a 15-page explanation of the council's judgement, and the evidence they had acquired made for damning reading. There were two hundred and eighty-eight text messages and thirty-five telephone calls between the sacked Stepney and the suspended Coughlan, the latter then passing on the illicitly obtained intelligence to Alonso and de la Rosa, covering five key technical areas: car weight distribution, flexible wing and aero balance, tyre gas, braking system, and strategy.

Amid all of this controversy, Hamilton was asked to change out of the sharp suit that he wore for the Paris meeting and back into his race outfit for a free

RIGHT: No hard feelings? Max Mosley shakes hands with Ron Dennis outside the McLaren hospitality unit after Saturday's qualifying at the Belgian Grand Prix.

LEWIS HAMILTON

PREVIOUS PAGE: Hamilton leads, but only in the pit-lane exit during qualifying at Spa-Francorchamps.

practice that saw him record the second-fastest time of the day – he was beaten to the top time by a tenth of a second by his teammate.

From the rookie's point of view, it was business as usual. 'The team are just as enthusiastic as always,' he insisted. 'We went through the usual programme today. It's quite easy to focus on the job. If anything, it's harder for the team, but they are doing a great job. As for me, my job is simple. I'm here to win.'

This goal appeared to be on the optimistic side after Saturday's official qualifying session. McLaren might have dominated the Italian Grand Prix in Monza the weekend before, but one week later and it was Ferrari's turn to hit back once again in this topsy-turvy season. For the first time that year, they secured the first two places on the grid, with Räikkönen finishing just 0.017 seconds ahead of Massa. Alonso claimed third, with Hamilton, believed to have qualified with the heaviest fuel load, back down in fourth.

'I love this circuit, and we have definitely improved the car since we tested here in July,' Hamilton explained. 'My final lap was really good today, with no mistakes. We haven't been quite as quick as the Ferraris, but victory is always a possibility, and I'm pretty confident I have a strong race strategy.'

Remarkably, he seemed unaffected by the week's traumatic events. 'I felt it was important to show my support for the team in Paris,' he explained. 'It hasn't affected my preparations, though. My pre-race schedule was a little more hectic than usual, but it hasn't been a distraction.' Hamilton was then asked how he had not become embroiled in the email exchanges between McLaren's other drivers, which had led to Thursday's stringent penalties. 'It's just one of those things that didn't really involve me,' he answered. 'I don't have Fernando's email address and haven't exchanged messages with Pedro since the Malaysian Grand Prix – and that was an email about a female.'

Late that afternoon, McLaren held another media briefing in their expensive motorhome. Alonso refused to discuss anything except qualifying. 'I'm here to race and will only talk about qualifying,' he announced. Dennis was more forthcoming, however. 'Once I became aware that new evidence might exist in the spying row, which I did on the morning of the Hungarian Grand Prix, I immediately phoned the FIA to keep them informed,' he said. 'Fernando and

I had a discussion in Hungary, but I'm not going to give you the details. When he left, I phoned the FIA to tell them what had happened. Half an hour later, his manager told me that Fernando was sorry and wanted to retract everything he'd said. Then, after the race, Fernando came to me, apologised, shook my hand and said, "Let's get on with racing." I accepted that.'

Max Mosley revealed that same afternoon what the world's media had already exposed. 'Ron rang me on the morning of the Hungarian Grand Prix and told me Alonso had some information he was threatening to give to the federation,' he confirmed.

Dennis, though, was still shaken by the World Motor Sport Council's verdict. 'Everything they disclosed is true,' he readily admitted. 'It happened, but I don't believe the facts are proportionate with the fine. If we don't appeal, it's because we want closure, and I hope the other teams will understand that we're swallowing a financial penalty in the interests of the sport. It won't be an admission that we've done anything wrong. The important thing is the company's integrity and the belief that we have never competed using another team's intellectual property.'

By the end of the following afternoon, he had a more familiar problem to deal with after another incident-packed Grand Prix, and once again his two warring drivers were at the centre of it. It was Ferrari's day, with Räikkönen and Massa producing a third one–two of the season. Although Massa appeared to be just about out of the title race, the Finn was edging himself closer and closer into contention.

After being second best in front of their adoring fans at Monza the week before, and with McLaren labelled as cheats to boot, victory for Ferrari in Belgium was sweet, especially as it mathematically confirmed them as the 2007 constructors' champions, with McLaren now out of the reckoning. Once again, though, after a race that for once that season resembled a procession, the main talking point was what went on behind the two Ferraris in the McLarens. As the cars hurtled down towards the first hairpin, 'La Source', the Spaniard veered across Hamilton's path and pushed him wide as they came out of the turn. The manoeuvre forced the rookie over the kerb, through the grass and onto the tarmac on the other side. Luckily for Hamilton, this took place at Spa. If it had been any other circuit, he may well have crashed into a wall. Instead, he kept

FACING PAGE: Final preparations – Hamilton makes final checks before driving in the Belgian Grand Prix.

his composure, steered his way back onto the track and continued with the race. The incident, though, effectively stopped him from mounting any serious challenge, and he trailed in fourth behind the third-placed Alonso for the rest of the Grand Prix. It meant that his lead at the top of the drivers' table, which had been as many as fourteen points at Magny-Cours in July, was now reduced to just two.

It then emerged immediately after the race that Alonso had offered his side of the McLaren garage a £10,000-per-race performance bonus – which worked out as £650 for each of his 15 men – if they could help make his car perform better.

Alonso later tried to defend his questionable manoeuvre on the track by blaming Massa's locked front wheel, insisting that the Brazilian had denied him space. Hamilton was having none of it. 'The last

few years I have been watching Formula One and Fernando has always been complaining about other people being unfair,' he said. 'Well, it was blatant. He quite deliberately pushed me wide. For someone who is trying to set a standard, he is not living up to it. There was enough room for both of us to get round, but suddenly I didn't have any room. It was not a fair race manoeuvre. I was lucky there was a run-off area.'

His lead was now down to just two points, but Hamilton insisted he remained confident. 'I don't fear anyone,' he said. 'I will just keep on pushing. The gap is closing, but there are still three races left, and I am still leading the championship.'

This was true, but suddenly, as the Formula One circus left European shores for the last time in 2007 and headed back east to first Japan and then China, Hamilton was not only having to look over

RACE RESULT

	DRIVER	TEAM	POINTS
1	Kimi Räikkönen	Ferrari	10
2	Felipe Massa	Ferrari	8
3	Fernando Alonso	McLaren-Mercedes	6
4	Lewis Hamilton	McLaren-Mercedes	5
5	Nick Heidfeld	BMW Sauber	4
6	Nico Rosberg	Williams	3
7	Mark Webber	Red Bull	2
8	Heikki Kovalainen	Renault	1

CONSTRUCTORS' CHAMPIONSHIP AFTER FOURTEEN RACES

	TEAM	POINTS
1	Ferrari	161
2	BMW Sauber	90
3	Renault	39
4	Williams	28
5	Red Bull	18
6	Toyota	12
7	Super Aguri	4
8	Honda	2

DRIVERS' CHAMPIONSHIP AFTER FOURTEEN RACES

	DRIVER	POINTS
1	Lewis Hamilton	97
2	Fernando Alonso	95
3	Kimi Räikkönen	84
4	Felipe Massa	77
5	Nick Heidfeld	56
6	Robert Kubica	33
7	Heikki Kovalainen	22
8	Giancarlo Fisichella	17
9	Nico Rosberg	15
10	Alex Wurz	13
11	Mark Webber	10
12	David Coulthard	8
13	Jarno Trulli	7
14	Ralf Schumacher	5
15	Takuma Sato	4
16	Jenson Button	2
17	Sebastian Vettel	1

ABOVE: It's Alonso from Hamilton at Spa-Francorchamps, but they have to make do with third and fourth behind the two Ferraris.

his shoulder for Alonso, but also for Räikkönen, who was timing a late but potentially winning run to the chequered flag. The understated Finn certainly saw it that way. 'It was a perfect result for the team,' he announced, happy with his weekend's work. 'We haven't given up. We are still in the hunt. We have reduced the gap, and there are three races to go. It would be amazing to do it, and we'll have to wait and see. But anything can happen.' After 14 of the most controversy-riddled Grands Prix in the history of the sport, nobody was about to disagree with him.

Race 15

Japanese Grand Prix

Oyama

Sunday, 30 September 2007

Attendance: 282,000 for the complete race weekend
Weather: heavy rain, 17 °C
Track temperature: 22 °C
Number of laps: 67
Circuit length: 2.835 miles
Race distance: 189.945 miles
Fastest lap: Lewis Hamilton, 1:28.193 (lap 27)

Hamilton 1st, 10 points (107)

FUJI SPEEDWAY

It had been quite a fortnight on and around the circuits at Monza and Spa, and now Hamilton, with his lead reduced to a precarious two points, faced three remaining Grands Prix to decide whether he could really complete the deal and make Formula One history. Just to make matters even more difficult, the next two races were in the Far East, while the denouement was due take place in Brazil. This meant racing on opposite sides of the world, with huge time differences, and with the weight of the world's expectations on his young, inexperienced shoulders.

Standing against him was his own teammate. Fernando Alonso had been there and done it – twice before. He was the man with the experience, and having reined in his young upstart of a team colleague's lead from fourteen to just two points over the course of the previous six races he was poised, like the athlete sitting on the shoulder of the race leader as they both hit the final bend in an Olympic final, to make his final move. The Spaniard had shown that he would stop at nothing to get his way, which made him a very dangerous opponent. Moreover, Kimi Räikkönen had made it known that as far as he was concerned the world title was still on the cards for

Ferrari as well. The world was closing in on Lewis Hamilton.

'I have still got the points advantage,' the 22 year old was quick to remind people. 'I think I just need to refocus myself for the last three races. It has been a fast and intense season. In the last two races, Fernando has done a fantastic job. I don't know if that is going to be the way it is going to be for the rest of the season. I need to pull my socks up, I guess. You have to experience losing as much as you do winning. I just haven't done as well as everybody else recently, that's all. I appreciate it has come down to two points, but we have still got three races and some tracks that are a bit new and fresh to everyone. On some circuits, he will be faster than me, and on some tracks I will be faster than him. So, fingers crossed the last tracks are better for me.'

He may have been under pressure, but at least he was happy with his team, and especially his boss. The same could not be said for Alonso. The week before the Japanese Grand Prix, more evidence from the World Motor Sport Council's hearing in Paris emerged, including the staggering revelation that Alonso and Dennis had not exchanged words for six weeks! The McLaren boss told the World Motor Sport Council,

'We are not on speaking terms. In Fernando's mind, there is the firm belief that our policy, whereby each driver receives equal treatment, does not properly reflect his status as world champion.'

As has already been documented, the problem that had been simmering all season finally blew up at the Hungarian Grand Prix after Alonso's demotion down the grid following qualifying. It was there that the Spaniard had made some threats to his boss, which had led to Dennis contacting the FIA. 'In that discussion, he was extremely upset with what had taken place the previous day, but nowhere near as upset as I was,' Dennis explained. 'He said things that he subsequently and fully retracted. He had also made a specific reference to emails from a McLaren engineer. When he made this statement, I said, "Stop!" I then went out and brought in chief operating officer Martin Whitmarsh, and Fernando said everything again in front of his manager. When he had finished, I turned to Mr Whitmarsh, asking what we should do with this particular part of the conversation. Martin said we should contact Max Mosley, FIA president. After Martin and Fernando left, that is exactly what I did. I recounted the entire conversation to Max. I was upset and angry, but mainly upset. Max calmed me down. He said that I should do nothing, and I started to calm down.

'Then, prior to the race, Fernando's manager came and said that Alonso had lost his temper and completely retracted everything he had said. When I phoned Max, he was understanding and said he would contact me prior to taking any action if he felt there was any real validity in what Fernando had said. Other than following up with Martin, the matter ended there until 26 days later when the drivers received a letter. What took place between those times, I do not know.'

Nigel Tozzi, Ferrari's lawyer, had asked Dennis at the hearing why he had not probed Alonso's original claims. 'We have not had any conversations since that point,' Dennis had replied. 'Alonso is not here because he does not want to be here. He does not speak to anyone much. He is a remarkable recluse for a driver. The relationship between Fernando and me is extremely cold. That is an understatement.'

In contrast, Hamilton had been in Paris, accompanied by his own legal team, which included Mark Phillips, QC. 'Lewis Hamilton has done nothing wrong,' Phillips had explained to the panel. 'He has won his points by driving. Gentlemen, when you come to consider what is fair, proportionate and just, we invite you to have in mind that the world wants to see the world's top drivers competing on track for the world championship.' Hamilton's counsel's closing remark might have played some part in the drivers being allowed to fight for the world championship. 'Let him get back to the track to become the first rookie world champion in Formula One history,' Phillips had continued. Despite the misgivings of several council members, and the admission afterwards by Bernie Ecclestone that both McLaren drivers had been 'minutes away' from exclusion, the plea had been heard and complied with.

Hamilton's season had been spared, but this was hardly his only problem as he arrived at Fuji, which had taken over the hosting of the Japanese Grand

Prix from Suzuka. His teammate's antics that season, particularly with regard to his involvement in the espionage affair that had proved so damaging to McLaren, and his move during the Belgian Grand Prix that could have been so damaging to Hamilton, caused the rookie to finally come out fighting. 'You try and understand people, but then the whole idea of what sort of a person they are is completely miles out of the ball park,' Hamilton explained on the Thursday before the race. 'He [Alonso] is not the person I imagined him to be, but that's the way it is. I came onto the scene with a bright, open mind. I thought, "Shoot, I'm here. I'm in Formula One." Then all the politics and stress surfaced – just so much stress. It was not what I expected, not what I was coming here to do. I was coming here to enjoy it, to race and compete. With everything that has gone on in the past couple of weeks, I think McLaren have started to realise who the real people are in the team and who they should really back. I feel my bond with the team is even stronger now. We arrived at Spa, and he [Alonso] was laughing and joking. I don't understand it.'

Despite this changed view of the double world champion, Hamilton's values remained intact. 'I want to win the right way,' he insisted. 'The best feeling ever is when you know you have beaten someone as talented as he is with the same equipment and opportunity. Not once have I approached the team and asked to be favoured. It is just not something I have done at any team, asking for better equipment. It is better when you both have equal opportunity.'

BELOW: Hamilton exits the pit lane at Fuji prior to qualifying. It is the start of a perfect weekend for the rookie.

The fact that Alonso had been attempting to pay off McLaren employees to produce a better car for him clearly irked Hamilton. 'It shows how much of a threat I am and that he is worried, which is great,' he observed. 'I don't understand why he would ask for favours.' However dubious Alonso's tactics had been, they seemed to have worked, and Hamilton was totally aware of the looming threat and what he was required to do about it. 'I have been working hard since the last race to understand where I have been losing time,' he admitted. 'I have a feeling that this weekend will be better than the previous few. I am feeling very confident and relaxed. I came out here early to be a bit of a tourist, to take my mind off things and prepare for a new attack, a fresh approach. It would be gutting to lose it now, so close to the end. I just have to do the job. I have to get out there and be faster than him in practice. The mental effect starts tomorrow morning. If I'm ahead of him, it starts churning up in his mind. I have to keep on being there. My aim is to do that to him.' Hamilton was concerned, however, about the tactics Alonso might use during the forthcoming race, especially after Spa. 'I will be a lot more aware of him around me,' he admitted. 'You wait and see. I'm driving to keep the car on the track and be fair to everyone. If that's how aggressive he wants to be, then I can be just as aggressive. But I'm not going to take silly risks and take myself or anyone else off. I just have to make sure I'm ahead of him so that it won't be an issue.'

As Hamilton was saying this, Alonso was sitting at a table just a few feet away, holding court. He appeared far from perturbed. 'For next year, I have a contract with this team, and I don't see any problem,' he said. 'I am fighting for the world championship, so everything is going quite well for me. I'm happy.'

He might not have been so happy if his burning ears had caught the final part of Hamilton's conference. 'Fernando is with his group, and there is my family, and they are very separate,' the rookie added. 'We tried our best to bring them together, and at one point it looked like they didn't want to know. Then we spoke to each other in Turkey, and it seemed to go a lot better. Then Spa happened. People said when you get to Formula One there will be a lot of sharks. I got here, and at the start I thought people were really nice. Clearly, not always.'

ABOVE: Happy days! Hamilton has just grabbed pole in qualifying in Japan. He is on his way to another Grand Prix victory.

ABOVE: The safety car leads – appalling conditions at Fuji led to the safety car being utilised for the first 19 laps of the race. Hamilton follows close behind.

One man who was extremely happy with the feud, the rivalry, the tension and the end-of-season showdown was Bernie Ecclestone, and the billionaire made no bones about it. The season had been the most remarkable for a decade, the emergence of Hamilton had lifted his sport just when it needed it and Ecclestone's dream of the season going right down to the wire was becoming more and more of a reality. He even had no qualms about contemplating the possibility of the two McLaren drivers taking one another out in the race. 'Like the $100-million fine, it would generate a lot of publicity,' he said, revealing his *raison d'être*. 'Imagine if that happened on the last lap of the last race. The guy who was leading at the time, points-wise, would be the winner. So, it would be a controversial end. I think he [Alonso] tried to take him [Hamilton] off in Belgium, didn't he? Well, it looked like it.'

He was extremely happy with his lot after overseeing the best part of the most exciting and controversial season for a decade or more. Now, with the season careering towards a wonderful climax, Ecclestone's wishes were coming true. Whatever the permutations were, it all made for good reading as far as he was concerned. 'Lewis is obviously good – the new kid on the block,' he surmised. 'If in his first year he comes into Formula One and wins a world title, it would be wonderful.' Alonso making it a hat-trick of successive world titles would be a decent tale, too, as would Kimi Räikkönen's amazing comeback in a Ferrari. Whatever the case, Ecclestone saw himself and his sport as the winners. 'All these outcomes are good,' he admitted. 'I don't think there's anything negative in any of them.'

On the Friday at free practice, the clouds lifted, and drivers and spectators caught a first glimpse of the spectacular Mount Fuji, which dominated the surrounding landscape. The track was staging its first Grand Prix in thirty years after the Ferrari driven by the late Gilles Villeneuve had crashed into the crowd, killing two, in 1977. The year before, James Hunt had won the world title for Britain in the driving rain.

Friday was also the day when Hamilton got back on track, literally and metaphorically speaking.

He dominated his teammate for all but the last few remaining laps of the morning session, and then set the fastest time of the day during the afternoon. Hamilton looked like a man on a mission. The math, as they say, was simple: finish ahead of Alonso and on the podium in the last three races of the season and the world title would be his.

This goal looked to be on track in the next day's qualifying session when Hamilton seized pole position, pipping Alonso in the process, and, as usual, he made sure it was achieved in dramatic fashion – and in dramatic conditions. Back in 1976, Fuji's inaugural Formula One Grand Prix took place in a blanket of fog and spray. The conditions were so bad that Niki Lauda, back from the crash that had burned him so badly, had refused to race, thus handing the world title to Hunt. They were not much better 31 years later. The poor conditions meant that all but the final few minutes of morning free practice were cancelled. As a result, the drivers did not do any serious wet-weather running until qualifying began in earnest, and Hamilton, caught up in all the mist and traffic, only just managed to squeeze into the second session.

'That was nerve-racking,' Ron Dennis admitted. 'The track was very busy, and Lewis seemed to be constantly surrounded by slower cars.'

Hamilton's last lap, however, was good enough for him to make the cut, and he went on to record the fastest laps in the second and final qualifying sessions, although he cut it fine to gain pole. Lying third, he dived back into the pits for a fresh set of wet tyres and just had enough time for one flying lap. It was all he needed. Hamilton improved by four-tenths of a second to beat Alonso by 0.07 seconds. 'I wasn't really aware which position I was in,' Hamilton said. 'It wasn't like normal qualifying when you just do one lap and come back in again. You had to stay out to try to improve in changing conditions. I knew I only had one opportunity to take pole, but I also had fresher tyres, plus the experience of my previous laps, so I knew where I could make up time. Looking at the data, it's clear I could have been quicker still, so it's good to know there's potentially even more to come.'

BELOW: Hamilton leads with Alonso barely visible behind due to the spray from the rain-lashed circuit in Japan. The Spaniard later crashed out of the race.

LEWIS HAMILTON

Both he and Alonso were aware of the looming threat Räikkönen presented. 'We're not idiots,' the Spaniard insisted. 'And we know how important it is to finish.' Hamilton knew he would have to watch the Finn and his own teammate. 'I've just got to be very careful,' he added. 'I need to be sharp to judge situations on the track and must be very aware of Fernando, because he's a big threat.'

A threat, maybe, but not a person Hamilton respected any more or even wanted to be teammates with. His relationship with the double world champion had slumped to the point that Hamilton admitted at Fuji that he did not want to be racing alongside Alonso the following season. 'I don't see how we can be teammates next season,' Hamilton said. 'I don't know who else would slip in here, but I'd rather it were Fernando in a Ferrari and me in a McLaren. It's up to the team. They've got to be smart and think about it. I know they've got politics and sponsors and all that sort of stuff. But they've got to do what's right, and I'm sure they will. He has stunned not only me, but everyone else, but he seems happier than ever. If the team want to keep him, they will, but I'm here to stay as long as they want me. The dreams that I have had about what I would like to be doing ten years in the future have slightly changed this season. It

has reconfirmed in my mind where I want to be and where I want to live out my career, and that is here.'

Hamilton also questioned whether Alonso, in his desperation to hold on to his world title, might resort to the kind of tactics that had tainted Michael Schumacher's glittering career. The German collided with Damon Hill in 1994 and again with Jacques Villeneuve in 1997 when the championship was on the line. 'I think it will be interesting to see during the last races whether he'll have the thing Schumacher had,' Hamilton said. 'Will he do absolutely anything and not care whether he runs himself or anyone else on the grid off the road? I guess that's one of the questions. And will he break under pressure? We'll just have to wait and see. But it will ruin his reputation more than mine, because I'd never do that. I want to win this fair and square. I still respect Alonso for what he has achieved. It takes a real driver to win consecutive world championships. He's extremely talented, but it's not just a question of going out there with talent. He's obviously done a lot of hard work in the background. I know things have been getting quite close during the last couple of races, but by no

BELOW: Need a hand? A course marshal helps a disenchanted Alonso out of his car after the Spaniard crashes out of the Japanese Grand Prix.

means do I feel it's over. It isn't at all. The battle is still very much on. It's easy to say, "I've just got to do a better job than him", but I really feel I can.'

Ron Dennis was clearly nervous about his drivers' spat spilling over onto the track. 'All the drivers' efforts should be focused on doing their job and competing fairly against each other,' he felt it fit to point out. 'They will both get an equal opportunity to win the world championship. I'm not wasting energy on anything else, and neither should they.'

Hamilton clearly heeded these words. The following afternoon, he produced what was undoubtedly the drive of his life to win the Japanese Grand Prix, his fourth win in his inaugural season in Formula One. The rain-soaked conditions made driving hazardous and had a major bearing on the final placings, which had a very strange look to them when compared with the rest of the season. Renault's Heikki Kovalainen claimed second, the first podium finish for the talented young Finn in his Formula One career, David Coulthard was fourth and Adrian Sutil was promoted from ninth to eigth after Vitantonio Liuzzi was handed a 25-second penalty. Of the title challengers,

Räikkönen finished third, but Alonso spun off into a wall on lap 42. It all meant that Hamilton now led the world drivers' championship by twelve points with just two Grands Prix remaining. The title would belong to the rookie if he won at the Chinese Grand Prix, the penultimate race of the season, or at least finished ahead of Alonso and Räikkönen.

It was a masterclass in the wet by Hamilton. While everyone else struggled in the slippery conditions, the British driver made no mistakes, leading from start to finish, save for his pit stops. The rain and fog made conditions so bad that the first 19 laps were conducted behind the safety car. Then, on lap 27, Alonso slipped off the track as he re-emerged from the pit lane, allowing Hamilton to make his own pit stop and rejoin the race still in front. A slight collision with Robert Kubica on lap 35 prompted him to back off to let cars that still had to make a second pit stop pass him by, rather than risk a crash.

Alonso, in contrast, had his car clipped by Sebastian

Vettel and then aquaplaned into a wall at turn five. While Alonso was returned to the garages by scooter, the safety car came out again so that debris from his McLaren could be cleared off the track. And with that, Hamilton was able to complete the race under no pressure whatsoever and afterwards spoke with justifiable pride. 'It was the best drive of my career,' he announced. 'During the last lap, I was thinking back to some of the races Ayrton Senna and Alain Prost were in. It makes me feel as if I'm on the way to achieving something similar to them. When I was a kid, I hoped that one day I'd be leading in torrential rain and pulling away by a second a lap. I was doing that. It made me feel so happy.

'It's a big boost in terms of confidence and my drive to be world champion. I really need to knuckle down now. I won't be partying tonight. The title is in the back of my mind, subconsciously, and the key is to focus on the next race and do the best job I can. I hope we have the pace to win again. I couldn't have imagined four wins in my first year. It's way, way beyond what I could have hoped for.'

Alonso admitted afterwards that he now faced a tough battle to keep hold of his world title. 'I'm not throwing in the towel, but unless there is a retirement from Hamilton we have to be realistic and say it's very hard to recover six points per race,' he said.

Räikkönen, who could still be champion, at least mathematically, was less than enamoured of his third place, especially after Ferrari claimed that the race stewards failed to inform them that all cars had to start on extreme-wet tyres. The Ferraris began with standard wets and were called in on lap three to make a mandatory change as a result. 'My race was ruined by the enforced pit stop,' Räikkönen insisted later. 'Clearly, the situation in the championship is a lot more difficult, but I will give it my all, right up to the very end.'

So too, though, would Lewis Hamilton, and it was left to Anthony to underline this point as he and his son started making plans for China. 'Although we've won today, you've got to wait until you've brought it home. Then it's all different. If you start celebrating now, you could end up with egg on your face. It's great, not just for us, but for everybody: the UK, the world and everybody who just likes underdogs in sport. I think Lewis will be buzzing tonight, but when he wakes up he'll be back to normal.' Lewis Hamilton was so close to making sporting history that he could almost touch it, but there was a nasty sting in the tail to come.

RACE RESULT			
	DRIVER	TEAM	POINTS
1	Lewis Hamilton	McLaren-Mercedes	10
2	Heikki Kovalainen	Renault	8
3	Kimi Räikkönen	Ferrari	6
4	David Coulthard	Red Bull	5
5	Giancarlo Fisichella	Renault	4
6	Felipe Massa	Ferrari	3
7	Robert Kubica	BMW Sauber	2
8	Adrian Sutil	Spyker	1

CONSTRUCTORS' CHAMPIONSHIP AFTER FIFTEEN RACES		
	TEAM	POINTS
1	Ferrari	170
2	BMW Sauber	92
3	Renault	51
4	Williams	28
5	Red Bull	23
6	Toyota	12
7	Super Aguri	4
8	Honda	2
9	Spyker	1

DRIVERS' CHAMPIONSHIP AFTER FIFTEEN RACES		
	DRIVER	POINTS
1	Lewis Hamilton	107
2	Fernando Alonso	95
3	Kimi Räikkönen	90
4	Felipe Massa	80
5	Nick Heidfeld	56
6	Robert Kubica	35
7	Heikki Kovalainen	30
8	Giancarlo Fisichella	21
9	Nico Rosberg	15
10	David Coulthard	13
10	Alex Wurz	13
12	Mark Webber	10
13	Jarno Trulli	7
14	Ralf Schumacher	5
15	Takuma Sato	4
16	Jenson Button	2
17	Sebastian Vettel	1
17	Adrian Sutil	1

ABOVE: This is becoming a habit – Hamilton has learned the art of spraying victory champagne after claiming his fourth win of the season at Fuji.

Race 16

Chinese Grand Prix

Shanghai

Sunday, 7 October 2007

Attendance: 150,000
Weather: light rain, 29 °C
Track temperature: 39 °C
Number of laps: 56
Circuit length: 3.387 miles
Race distance: 189.672 miles
Fastest lap: Felipe Massa, 1:37.454 (lap 56)

Hamilton DNF, 0 points (107)

SHANGHAI INTERNATIONAL CIRCUIT

Now twelve points behind his young teammate with just two races remaining, Fernando Alonso's mood was hardly positive as he started to make plans for China. Seemingly beaten to the championship by a rookie who had had the temerity to assassinate his character in front of the world's media in Japan, the least the double world champion could do was return the compliment, and this he duly did on Spanish radio, pointing out that if he was forced to stay at McLaren-Mercedes, the 2008 Formula One season would be as acrimonious as the 2007 season had been. 'I'd be delighted if I didn't carry on with Hamilton,' Alonso admitted. 'If we are not together next season and I can go to a good car, then great. If we have to carry on together, then we will have another great battle.'

Gossip was rife in the paddock concerning Alonso's future. Ferrari were supposedly interested, as were Renault, where Flavio Briatore had made no secret of his wish to bring his protégé back to the team that had helped him win back-to-back world titles. 'I've told Fernando that as soon as he is ready to leave McLaren, we will gladly take him back,' revealed the Italian team principal at Renault.

For the time being, Alonso was hedging his bets. 'It hasn't entered into my plans not to race next year,' he said. 'And I don't have any news about Ferrari. They have a contract with Kimi Räikkönen and Felipe Massa for next year. I have to concentrate on the last two races of this season. All I must think about is racing and winning at Shanghai and Interlagos [Brazil]. My retirement in Japan has not made it easy for me in the championship, but there are still 20 points to be won, and I am going to fight hard for each one of them.'

It was fair to say that the Hamilton family were not losing sleep over Alonso's future. Anthony, who doubled up as his son's manager, planned to sit down with Ron Dennis after the final Grand Prix of the season in Brazil to renegotiate his son's contract, and the pay rise would be substantial. In 2007, Hamilton earned a basic salary of £340,000, although a bonus of £7,000 extra for each championship point won meant that this figure had shot up to over £1 million. However, this paled into insignificance compared with what Hamilton could be earning in 2008. If he could finish the job in either China or Brazil and become world champion at the first

attempt, Hamilton could expect an annual salary of a staggering £10 million.

'We are in a long-term relationship,' said Anthony. 'At the moment we have no plans to escape, because McLaren are a good, honest team full of integrity, and we're happy here.' As for his son's meteoric rise, Anthony was well prepared. 'People ask, "Can you believe the hype?" That word has followed us around since Lewis was seven years old. But at every stage, we have proved that the word doesn't apply to us. We come along and try and do an honest job. There is no hype around Lewis. It's just decent, honest hard work.'

His son had more pressing matters on his mind, such as becoming world champion in Shanghai, but he was trying hard to maintain a low-key approach to what was undoubtedly the biggest race of his life. 'I will prepare exactly the same as I did in Japan,' he insisted. 'I will do a little bit of sightseeing around Shanghai. I find it easy to stay relaxed. After the previous race in Belgium, I went back to the factory

ABOVE: Alonso's next team – Renault boss Flavio Briatore observes from the grid, having already made public his invitation for his former driver Alonso to leave McLaren and return to Renault.

early because I wanted to figure out why things were not exactly right. I thought, "That's it. I've sorted it out." I then went to Japan and did a great job. I'm focused.'

Hamilton had indeed done a fantastic job in Japan. The best part of his victory was that it brought Alonso's gathering momentum, built up over the previous six races, to a shuddering halt. 'I have turned the momentum around against Fernando,' Hamilton explained. 'Everyone has been saying that Fernando had the momentum all of a sudden, and for me it was part of my inexperience. I didn't think that was the case. I just needed to figure out what was going on and put the pieces of the puzzle back together. I think I have done that. I never imagined I would come away from Japan with a 12-point lead. To get the ten points against Fernando was something I never thought I would do again this season.'

That said, he was extremely keen to play down talk of world titles, at least in Shanghai. He appreciated that he held a massive advantage but also knew that the pendulum in Formula One could swing rapidly and dramatically in the opposite direction. 'There has been a lot of talk over the last couple of days about the championship, but I just push that to the back of my mind,' Hamilton insisted. 'I am focused only on the next two races and doing the best I can in China and Brazil. The last two races of this season are at tracks that I have not been to before. I don't see that as a problem, as that has been the case on four occasions already this season – at Melbourne, Montreal, Indy and Fuji – and I was on the podium at all of those races. From what I understand of the Shanghai circuit, it is vast in comparison with Interlagos, so we will probably have two very different races. Everything is too tight for me to predict what will happen, but I feel well prepared to take on the challenge.'

The challenge was underlined on the Thursday before the Chinese Grand Prix when Hamilton came to realise just how much it had irked the egos of the other major drivers on the grid that a young man from GP2 had turned up and taken the championship by storm. Only one man in the driver line-up had won the world title – Alonso – and yet here was a rookie who was on the verge of making the achievement appear ridiculously easy.

Ideally, Hamilton would have liked to have spent that Thursday preparing for the hugely pressurised task that lay ahead of him that weekend at the Shanghai circuit. Instead, his victory and the ten points won in Japan were suddenly under threat because footage shot by a local fan in Fuji suggested that Hamilton had been driving erratically while the safety car was in operation on the track as rain came pelting down.

BELOW: A close shave – a relieved Hamilton with Ron Dennis in the Shanghai paddock after escaping any penalty for allegedly interfering with fellow drivers Mark Webber and Sebastian Vettel during the Japanese Grand Prix.

Taking the final bend on lap 46, the rookie lurched over to the right and suddenly reduced his speed. Sebastian Vettel, lying third in his Toro Rosso at the time, was so distracted by this that he hit Mark Webber's second-placed Red Bull, which had also been forced to slow down to avoid overtaking Hamilton, a move forbidden while the safety car is out on the circuit. Hamilton escaped any penalty for this at the time, but Vettel, blamed for the incident, was told that he would start the Chinese Grand Prix ten places down the grid as a result. However, a 19-second YouTube video became the major talking point in the garages and paddock in Shanghai, because it provided footage of the incident from a previously unseen angle. This played a key part in the investigation by the stewards, who planned to announce their verdict on the Friday. If they decided against the British driver, he could lose the ten points gained in Japan or be excluded from the Chinese Grand Prix.

His alleged offence was brought to light by Toro Rosso team principal Franz Tost, who approached the stewards after being made aware of the YouTube video. 'You could see quite clearly that Hamilton slows down quite unexpectedly,' said Tost. 'Sebastian [Vettel] would have had to have gone between the cars, and there was no chance of that. It was totally unexpected. It looked like Hamilton was stopping, which is why I went to the stewards.'

The driver of the safety car, senior FIA official Bernd Mayländer, let it be known in an unofficial briefing that he saw nothing wrong with Hamilton's actions, but this was not Webber's view. 'It definitely contributed to Sebastian hitting me, because Hamilton wasn't doing what he was supposed to be doing,' argued the Australian. 'He spoke in the drivers' meeting about how good a job he was going to do, and he did the opposite.'

Vettel was also less than amused. 'I saw Lewis move far to the right and thought he was coming to a stop,' he said. 'I obviously did not plan to ruin both races.'

Once again, Hamilton's pre-race preparations were proving to be far from ideal. Instead of completing a successful free practice day followed by a quiet evening, the rookie spent much of the night explaining himself to the race stewards. Sitting next to Webber and Vettel, he told his story and then, in the company of McLaren team manager Dave Ryan, put his case across. Footage of the incident was shown on a screen, and Hamilton then spoke in

his own defence. It did the trick. The stewards were convinced that he had done little wrong, especially in such treacherous conditions. They dismissed the case, freeing up Hamilton to take his 12-point lead into the penultimate Grand Prix of the season, and they also waived Vettel's punishment while they were at it.

In a statement, the stewards said, 'What has become apparent is the view clearly expressed by all drivers and team managers that the conditions at Fuji were exceptionally bad and worse than those previously experienced when the race started behind the safety car. Because of these views, the stewards accept that it may be inappropriate to impose the penalty normally applied for an offence such as this.'

There was a second sting in the tail waiting for Hamilton. Luca di Montezemolo, president of Ferrari, announced that if the rookie went on to win the world title, it would be tainted in light of the espionage scandal and the $100-million fine handed out to McLaren. Hamilton begged to differ. 'No,' he said. 'I came from the GP2 season and was finally given the opportunity in Formula One with the team I had always dreamed of being with. I finally got here, and I knew the guys so well and was confident in their abilities. There has been no need for them to cheat. I've seen how hard people work. I have no need to cheat. I'm not going to win the world championship because my car is much quicker than Ferrari's. We've had some tough battles, and we've done a better job with reliability. Some races Ferrari have won, and some races we've bounced back and beaten them. If we'd cheated, we'd have won every race. I've come to Shanghai knowing that the car has been put together by an honest group of guys working their arses off. So, there's nothing anyone can do or say to change the way I feel about the issue.'

At least the controversy occupied Hamilton's mind, which meant he did not have to think too much about the enormity of what he could achieve in Shanghai. However, the young driver insisted that he was not suffering from sleepless nights because of the pressure. 'I've been just as relaxed this week as I was last week,' he said. 'I don't know why that is. I don't have an answer. I'm just not worried. My preparation will be the same as it was in the last race. It was the best race of my life. And considering that I've only been out in the rain in a Formula One car a few times, I even

FACING PAGE: Man on a mission – Hamilton on his way to qualifying fastest in Shanghai from Kimi Räikkönen and Felipe Massa.

surprised myself. They were such tricky conditions that I was really happy with the way I coped. I showed that I'm not the rookie everyone expected me to be.'

This was a rare upbeat moment for Hamilton on a day he otherwise found difficult to deal with. For the first time all season, he appeared down and disillusioned with his sport. 'There have been some really strange situations this year, in which I've been made to look like the bad person,' he said. 'If this is the way it's going to keep going, it's not really somewhere I want to be. I had a good weekend in Japan, I didn't put a foot wrong and I didn't do anything to put anyone else in danger. Formula One's supposed to be about hard, fair competition. That's what I've tried to do this year – just be fair. People tried to blame me for Mark and Sebastian crashing. I was well out of the way. I wasn't driving an abnormal race. I was doing the same the whole race. There was more grip on that side. I've got to maintain my gap behind the safety car, and they've got to maintain their gap behind me. It's not my job to look after the people behind me. I couldn't see anything out of my visor, because there was water inside and my mirrors were all fogged up.'

If his mood was downbeat on the Friday night, it was much improved 24 hours later after he grabbed pole position for the Chinese Grand Prix, 0.136 seconds ahead of Kimi Räikkönen and 0.313 ahead of Felipe Massa. Fernando Alonso, Hamilton's nearest challenger, would be starting in fourth place on the grid. Yet still the events of the past couple of days ate away at him, especially the tirade he faced during the drivers' briefing. 'I went into the briefing on Friday night, and everyone had their rifles out ready to shoot me,' Hamilton revealed. 'That was interesting. It was strange, but I've had it plenty of times in my life. It was disappointing, because I know the drivers, and I didn't expect them to say certain things. But it won't deduct any joy from me becoming the next world champion. I didn't get here by luck. I've worked really hard, and so have the team. Any success we've got on the track, we've deserved.'

Despite this, he admitted that he had feared the worst when he had been summoned by the stewards. 'I immediately accepted I would get a penalty here – for what I didn't know – but I went in and told them my views. They came out for me, and I think it was the best decision, but I was quite relieved. I was able to get rid of that heavy bag off my shoulders. There's already a huge weight there from leading

the championship. It's been a bit of a roller coaster this weekend and quite an emotional period for me. I did put my hand up after yesterday, and perhaps I didn't do the best job under the safety car, but it was my first experience. I promised to do the best I could next time. This has been a mind-blowing season for me and for everyone in Formula One with everything that has gone on. It will be great to win the world championship, and if I don't this year, then I have many more years ahead of me.'

Hamilton also revealed yet more cause for motivation: a McLaren F1 LM sports car. A papaya-

ABOVE: It's in the bag ... isn't it? Hamilton celebrates after claiming pole at the Chinese Grand Prix to take what he believed to be a big step towards sealing the world title.

orange prototype, which Hamilton had his eye on, sat inside McLaren's Technology Centre in Woking. 'It has been my favourite car since I was about eight years old,' Hamilton admitted. 'I got a book for Christmas that year, and it had this orange car on the front. When I first went to McLaren aged 13, it was there. I just fell in love with it. Every time I go to the workshop in Woking, it's there.'

Ron Dennis had promised Hamilton the car – built to celebrate the team's debut victory at the Le Mans 24-hour race in 1995 – but it was not as simple as that. 'We've done a deal, but Lewis has got to win two

of the next three championships,' Dennis revealed. 'That gives me a bit of a time to save the car.'

If Hamilton was happy with his qualifying performance, Alonso, in fourth, was not. After he kicked a toilet door at the team's hospitality suite in the Shanghai paddock so hard that a carpenter had to be called in, he aimed another metaphorical boot at McLaren, and especially Ron Dennis, because he had failed to beat his teammate with similar fuel

ABOVE: So far, so good – Hamilton during the early stages of the Chinese Grand Prix, happily oblivious to the major problems that lay ahead.

loads. 'When I crossed the line, I was very happy with the lap. On the radio, they told me I was fourth, and I was surprised, because I thought I was nearly at the maximum,' he said. 'I said on the radio, "This is a good lap," and I expected to be fighting for the pole. Then I realised I was still fourth with an even bigger gap to pole. I was expecting a lot more from the team. It's better to be silent than to lie – and that's something he [Dennis] should do more often. Many of the scandals McLaren have been involved in off the track this year have been created by these things. I'm always angry when I'm not in a good position and don't perform as well as I can. I am frustrated, but I'm not thinking of this championship any more, because it has been decided off the track.' By this, he meant the stewards' decision not to dock his teammate points. 'You go there to hear what the officials say. Twenty-one drivers have an opinion and the officials another. It's like talking to a wall.'

With teammates like Alonso, Hamilton hardly needed any enemies. Still, as he prepared for what was potentially the biggest day of his life, he vowed he would not err on the cautious side. 'I don't see any reason to change my approach,' he said. 'If I'm playing golf and find myself stuck in the bushes, I don't play safe. I go straight for the green. I'll tackle the race as I always do – by aiming to win.'

That was the aim, but the reality proved to be very different indeed. The next day, and for the first time that season, Hamilton failed to finish the race after a rare but costly mistake, leaving the champagne still on ice and the eulogies held over, at least for another fortnight.

It all began well enough, with a clean start for the field on what was a damp track in Shanghai. All Hamilton had to do was keep ahead of Alonso, but when Räikkönen charged him on lap 28 the rookie's racing instinct took over, and the McLaren held the Ferrari at bay. Ron Dennis admitted afterwards that Hamilton had been the calmest man in the McLaren garage before the race, and when the pit-wall team instructed their driver to take it nice and easy he allowed Räikkönen through one lap later.

This is when the real drama began. Hamilton was on intermediate tyres, which were wearing thin and had lost him thirteen seconds to Alonso in just three laps. Hindsight says he should have switched to dry tyres, but McLaren were adamant that it was about to rain. By lap 31, his tyres had worn away

to virtually nothing, making his car very difficult to handle as a result, and Hamilton realised that he had to dive into the pits for the second time in the race.

Instead, he lost control on the pit-lane entry, slid to his right and came to a stop in the gravel. When the marshals arrived on the scene, Hamilton sat in his cockpit imploring them to help him get back onto the

track, but it was to no avail. With just 25 laps standing between him and the end of a race which would have confirmed him as world champion, Hamilton knew his biggest blunder of the season could not have happened at a worse time.

Räikkönen went on to win the Chinese Grand Prix, a victory that suddenly thrust him into contention for the world title, and with Alonso finishing second Hamilton's lead in the drivers' championship was down to four. The Spaniard was second, with one hundred and three points, and the Finn was three points behind

BELOW: Get me back on that track! Hamilton implores officials to help him get back into the Chinese Grand Prix after sliding off at the entrance to the pit lane.

him in third. All three would be going to the last Grand Prix of the season in Brazil with a shot at the title.

'I was gutted when I got out of the car,' Hamilton admitted. 'I hadn't made a mistake all year, and to do it on the way into the pits is not something I usually do. But you can't go through life without making mistakes. I'm over it. Now we look forward to Brazil, and I know the team is working hard to make sure the car is quick enough. There are still points to be had. I'm disappointed, but there is still one more race to go, and we are still ahead. I will bounce back and attack it.'

Those concerned were quick with their explanations when it came to the error of judgement concerning the tyres. 'The tyres were getting worse and worse, but my mirrors were dirty, and I couldn't see them,' Hamilton said. 'It's unfortunate for the team. They did a fantastic job as always, and I'm sorry for them. The decision to keep the intermediate tyres was a joint one between me and the team, and I didn't realise how badly damaged they were. It's all part of my learning process.'

The team management were keen to deflect the blame away from the rookie. 'I don't think we did anything dramatically wrong, and neither did Lewis,' Ron Dennis insisted. 'But the circuit was considerably drier than the pit-lane entrance. That's what made a difference.' Martin Whitmarsh went further. 'We are the ones with all the information,' he added. 'It was a lap too long. Hindsight is a wonderful thing.'

The smiles in the McLaren hospitality centre were conspicuous by their absence on the Sunday night in Shanghai. They could and maybe should have been celebrating history, courtesy of a rookie becoming the first-ever world champion. Instead, the next fortnight was about to seem like an eternity. Hamilton attempted to brighten the mood with his trademark optimism. 'Don't worry,' he said. 'We still have one race to go. I can still do it.' Of that there was no doubt, but suddenly, and quite unexpectedly, the race to become the world's best driver would all boil down to a three-man shoot-out at Interlagos, and the twenty-two-year-old Brit who had led the drivers' championship most of the way was in grave danger of being overtaken at the final bend of what had been an utterly compelling season.

RACE RESULT

	DRIVER	TEAM	POINTS
1	Kimi Räikkönen	Ferrari	10
2	Fernando Alonso	McLaren-Mercedes	8
3	Felipe Massa	Ferrari	6
4	Sebastian Vettel	Toro Rosso	5
5	Jenson Button	Honda	4
6	Vitantonio Liuzzi	Toro Rosso	3
7	Nick Heidfeld	BMW Sauber	2
8	David Coulthard	Red Bull	1

CONSTRUCTORS' CHAMPIONSHIP AFTER SIXTEEN RACES

	TEAM	POINTS
1	Ferrari	186
2	BMW Sauber	94
3	Renault	51
4	Williams	28
5	Red Bull	24
6	Toyota	12
7	Toro Rosso	8
8	Honda	6
9	Super Aguri	4
10	Spyker	1

DRIVERS' CHAMPIONSHIP AFTER SIXTEEN RACES

	DRIVER	POINTS
1	Lewis Hamilton	107
2	Fernando Alonso	103
3	Kimi Räikkönen	100
4	Felipe Massa	86
5	Nick Heidfeld	58
6	Robert Kubica	35
7	Heikki Kovalainen	30
8	Giancarlo Fisichella	21
9	Nico Rosberg	15
10	David Coulthard	14
11	Alex Wurz	13
12	Mark Webber	10
13	Jarno Trulli	7
14	Sebastian Vettel	6
14	Jenson Button	6
16	Ralf Schumacher	5
17	Takuma Sato	4
18	Vitantonio Liuzzi	3
19	Adrian Sutil	1

ABOVE: The dream begins to die – it's all down to Brazil after Hamilton retires in Shanghai and throws the world drivers' championship wide open.

Race 17

Brazilian Grand Prix

São Paulo

Sunday, 21 October 2007

Attendance: 70,000
Weather: sunny, 37 °C
Track temperature: 60 °C
Number of laps: 71
Circuit length: 2.677 miles
Race distance: 190.067 miles
Fastest lap: Kimi Räikkönen, 1:12.445 (lap 66)

Hamilton 7th, 2 points (109)

After a season that had begun in Australia in March and had included 16 races, taking the Formula One circus all over the globe, from Malaysia in South East Asia and Bahrain in the Middle East to the traditional circuits of Europe, such as Monaco, Silverstone and the Nürburgring, then on to North America, and Japan and China in the Far East, it would all come down to one final race. For three racing drivers, Brazil offered the opportunity for one of them to make history. For Lewis Hamilton, the leader in the race for the drivers' title, the chance to become the first-ever rookie world champion was one he was desperate to take. For Fernando Alonso, the second-placed driver, the possibility of winning a hat-trick of successive world titles was very real. And for Kimi Räikkönen, considered by many to be the fastest driver in the world, the most unlikely of comebacks was now on the cards. Someone would have to break. Someone would have to produce something extra. Only one of them would be smiling at the end of the weekend in Brazil.

As far as Hamilton was concerned, it would be him. By the time he touched down in London after the Chinese Grand Prix, he had erased any negative

memories from his shattering experience in Shanghai. 'I've been in these situations before many times, needing to close out championships, and I know how to deal with the situation,' he insisted. 'It's my first year in Formula One, but there is no reason why it should be different for me. My approach will be the same.'

So, no lasting damage from seeing a world title snatched away from him in China, then? 'If you start to reflect on negatives in this business, it can affect the way you think. When I think about getting into that car, there is nothing that gives me a better feeling. I try to enjoy my life. I'm really not complaining. Brazil is yet to come, so you shouldn't worry – I can still do it.'

The Brazilian Grand Prix was the first three-way title decider since 1986, when Nigel Mansell had famously seen his tyre blow at 180 mph with just seventeen laps remaining. Leading the world championship by six points from Alain Prost, the British racing icon had seen his world-title dream shattered with just forty-four miles of the season remaining. In total, three-way deciders had taken place on just eight occasions in the fifty-seven-year history of the Formula One world championship, with the pre-race leader triumphant only three times. Alonso would have taken great heart from the fact that the driver lying second before the final race went on to become world champion on four occasions, with the third-placed driver claiming the world title only once.

But the former British world champions were all backing Hamilton, especially Mansell, who admitted to still being haunted by what had happened in Adelaide 21 years earlier. 'At the time, it was horrible,' confessed the man who had gone on to become world champion in 1992. 'Even today, it's not nice to talk about. It was lap 65 in Adelaide when the rear-left tyre exploded. It took me nearly a quarter of a mile to bring the car under control. I was sitting comfortably in third, which was all I needed, and after a whole season it was down to the last race and the last 44 miles of that race. I was invited by the FIA to the end-of-season world championship awards in Paris. At the ceremony, I sat next to the clerk of the course. He asked me if I knew what would have happened if I had crashed, and I told him I would have broken my legs or worse. He replied, "If you'd crashed, there would have been debris all over the track, and the race would have been stopped. The rules stated that the race would not have restarted, because two-thirds of the distance had been covered so you would have been crowned world champion." So, I lost the world title twice in one day because I didn't know the rules.'

Mansell did not believe the same fate would befall Hamilton. 'Lewis is in a win–win situation,' he explained. 'If he becomes world champion – and I firmly believe he will – he will round off what has been an astounding first season in Formula One. If either Alonso or Räikkönen pips him in Brazil, then it has still been the most remarkable season ever by a rookie, and Hamilton will know, just as I did in 1986, that the world title has merely been delayed a year or two.'

Two knights of the realm also believed Hamilton would finish the job. 'What Lewis has done this year is quite remarkable,' said Sir Jackie Stewart. 'He's won four Grands Prix, he's been in pole positions, he's done fastest laps – it really is fairy-tale stuff. I think he'll do it. I think he's got the legs, and I think he's got the ability.'

Sir Stirling Moss, recognised by most to be the greatest driver never to have become world champion, agreed. 'It just means we have to wait another two weeks,' he said. 'Lewis deserves it, and now that it has gone down to the line he deserves a bonus. He is the

greatest driver around and probably ever. In my racing lifetime, I have never seen a driver get so far and do so well with such ease. If Hamilton doesn't win, I'll be terribly disappointed, but I think he'll pull it off.'

Damon Hill won the world title in 1996 but lost both the 1994 and 1995 title races by a single point to Michael Schumacher. 'Any time you are leader of the world championship going into the final race,

you have the upper hand,' he said. 'But, then again, there is qualifying to get through, there are all sorts of unforeseen complications and two other guys in the title hunt as well. It is going to be a fearsome battle going into the final round. It's tremendously exciting for the sport. It has been a fantastic season all the way through, with great racing and the emergence of a real superstar in Lewis Hamilton.'

ABOVE: Hamilton and Alonso fool nobody as they try to make out all is well between them on the eve of the Brazilian Grand Prix.

Still, Hamilton had to fight against highly accomplished challengers in Brazil, one of whom was a teammate who would be the last person to help him out. At least Räikkönen would have the support of Felipe Massa, who would finish fourth in the drivers' championship no matter what happened in Brazil.

'If Kimi has a chance during the race to win the championship, I think it's very good for the team, and I would be very happy to help him,' Massa promised. 'If maybe Lewis or Fernando are in the middle and we have no chance, then I will try to win the race.'

After a week relaxing at home, playing some golf, running with his personal trainer and just chilling out, Hamilton was in a more reflective mood about what had happened in Shanghai and what needed to happen in Brazil. Indeed, he accepted that his impetuous nature had perhaps got the better of him when it had mattered most. 'We were in a perfect position to win the championship,' he admitted. 'But I wanted to win the race. I was out there driving for the win. Things like that can happen. You can learn from that situation. Though I believe we have to go to Brazil thinking in terms of winning the race, starting from pole and leading from the start, some part of the mind has to be focused on the end result. I understand the position I'm in and what I need to do. We can't take risks, that's for sure. Maybe I did take a risk at the last race.'

This was an acceptance of a mistake in an otherwise perfect season, but Hamilton was quick to turn a negative into a positive. 'If anything, I'm mentally stronger,' he insisted. 'Other drivers might be on the back foot and struggling after experiencing something like that. But I have taken the negatives and turned them into a positive. I'm four points ahead. I just need to go out there and do a good job.

'I think I have done pretty well all year in terms of finishing in good positions. For any driver, it is a hard hit knowing that it was there and you didn't take it. But it has been an amazing season. Who would have thought I'd be challenging for the world championship. And after a DNF [did not finish], I'm still leading the championship with a good chance of winning it. It's still pretty cool. I'm in the best position to win in Brazil in a good car that should suit the circuit.'

In any case, some observers, especially in Spain, believed that Hamilton had the advantage, because McLaren would favour him. This opinion stemmed from the treatment that Alonso believed he had been forced to endure, on and off, all season. The double world champion distanced himself from such theories when he arrived in Brazil. 'I'm sure we're going to Brazil with full equality across the team and two cars capable of fighting for victory in the race and in the championship,' said the Spaniard. 'Although I am now only four points away from Lewis, I still need for there to be a lot of circumstances in my favour that are out of my control. I have to do my bit, then hope everything else falls into place.'

But the whispering continued, to the extent that McLaren saw fit to issue a statement. 'We can categorically state that they [the drivers] will be given the exact same opportunity to win the race and the championship,' stated chief executive Martin Whitmarsh. 'Both drivers have held these positions for the majority of the year, and every single member of the team is pushing hard for the victor to be one of our two drivers.'

By the Thursday before the Brazilian Grand Prix, both McLaren drivers were trying their hardest to convince the world that their relationship had improved. 'People have said many things about us, but they are untrue,' said Alonso in a statement that was met with a degree of incredulity by the world's media. 'We never had any problems with each other. We are obviously fighting on the track, but off the track we have had a very good relationship from day one, so it's still the same.'

Whatever he said, a move away from McLaren was still the most likely scenario for Alonso. With Ferrari confirming Räikkönen and Massa as their two drivers for the following season, and with Alonso turning down a staggering offer of £25 million a year from Toyota – which would have more than doubled his salary – Renault appeared to be the favoured destination for the Spaniard.

Hamilton, meanwhile, attempted to join in the unlikely truce. 'I think our relationship is as good as ever,' he said. 'I think we've got on quite well all year, despite what the media have said.' He was a lot more convincing when he turned to the subject of his state of mind now that he was actually in Brazil. In China, he had clearly been on edge. In Brazil, despite it all coming down to the final race, Hamilton felt much more at ease. 'I don't know why, but I feel confident,' he said. 'Hopefully, it will be a good weekend, but, equally, I know it could be a bad one. In the end, the result in China took the pressure off my shoulders. I came out of it even stronger. I thought it would knock my confidence and put me on the back foot.

FACING PAGE: Kimi Räikkönen, the least favoured to become world champion in Brazil, in discussion with Lewis Hamilton after qualifying saw the Finn finish third and the Briton second behind Felipe Massa.

But it was a good learning experience. Coming here, I feel a lot different compared to the last race. All the pressure was building up, and there was a lot happening on the Thursday and Friday. It wasn't a great weekend. Now I feel totally relaxed. All this is beyond my imagination. This is what I have worked for all my life. The first win this season is still the most memorable. Even then, some people had some doubts about me, but I knew I could do it. I have fire in my heart.'

Back home in Britain, and especially in England, the sporting public were in for a rare and privileged treat. The England rugby union team had, against all predictions, reached a World Cup final against South Africa that would take place on the Saturday of the Brazilian Grand Prix weekend. Then, one day later, Hamilton was going for a first British world title in Formula One for eleven years. Hamilton, like many others back home, had been caught up in the rugby euphoria. 'It's one of the best times for our country,' he said. 'I am pleased and proud to be in a position where I can do something. I really want England to win. I watched the last game, and I had a great time with a few friends. It was amazing to see the spirit of the England guys.'

However, Hamilton's own spirit took a knock during Friday's free practice, and the potential repercussions were massive. He was called before the race stewards in the afternoon to answer why he had used two sets of wet-weather tyres rather than the stipulated one set during the day's first practice session. This, of course, was not his error, but it most certainly was a massive mistake by McLaren, and it could have cost Hamilton the world title. The fear was that the young driver could be demoted down the grid for such a crime, and with the destiny of the world title hanging in the balance such a penalty would have been decisive. Instead, as dusk fell in São Paulo, the stewards decided to fine McLaren 15,000 euros (£10,500) and remove one set of tyres from Hamilton's stock for that weekend. 'It was 100 per cent our fault, not Lewis's,' admitted Ron Dennis that night. 'Perhaps we were too tense. We're trying so hard, but it was a silly mistake. We can do no more than our best. People make mistakes. It perhaps shows that we are all human.'

RIGHT: Ferrari flyer – Felipe Massa gets away quickest from pole, with Ferrari teammate Kimi Räikkönen cruising past Lewis Hamilton to take second place. Fernando Alonso is also about to leapfrog Hamilton into third.

PREVIOUS PAGE: Showing his age – Lewis Hamilton responds to being overtaken by Fernando Alonso by running wide off the track at turn four, a mistake that cost him two places on the first lap of the Brazilian Grand Prix.

Reprieved and relieved, Hamilton was able to enjoy the fact that he was at the home of his hero Ayrton Senna, about to race at the famous Interlagos circuit with the world title almost within touching distance in his rookie year. Moreover, the Brazilians, whose love for motor racing is matched only by their love of football, had taken Hamilton to their hearts. Already he had earned the nickname 'Robinho', after the young Brazil and Barcelona football star, and with his coloured skin and modest background, the locals in the sprawling city of São Paulo knew a role model when one came along.

'It's quite surreal being here,' Hamilton admitted. 'For many years, I've wanted to come to Brazil and race at Interlagos. I'm buzzing. I can't wait. I've had a phenomenal season for my first year in Formula One. I'm 22 and very, very fortunate to be driving for McLaren. Now I have the chance to win the world championship this weekend. If I do, then it will be fantastic. It will be a big step in my career and my life. If not, then I'll live to fight another day, and I'll move on to next year and try to win it then.'

He was trying desperately hard not to get ahead of himself, but he did let slip one plan he had up his sleeve, and that was to copy his hero Senna and unfurl a Union Jack from his car if he finished the Grand Prix as world champion. 'It would be pretty cool,' Hamilton admitted. 'You see Valentino Rossi doing it on his motorbike, and it does so much for the sport. It brings you closer to the people. If someone gives me a flag and I've won the race, then, sure, I'd do that.'

He took what appeared to be a major step towards fulfilling his dream the following afternoon when he qualified in second place on the grid for the Brazilian Grand Prix, but not before yet more controversy clouded the day. As the season took another twist on its penultimate day, the British driver had to defend himself against accusations of cheating. Having recorded the second-best lap behind pole winner Felipe Massa, Hamilton was accused of impeding Kimi Räikkönen during the Finn's flying lap. Hamilton was on an 'out-lap' at the time and appeared to move out of the way only at the very last moment. 'I came out of the pit lane, and the team said, "You will be coming close to Kimi." At that speed, your mirrors are vibrating and you can't see. I apologise if I got in his way, but I didn't think he was that close to me. I stayed where I was and braked. I didn't feel I hindered his lap, and I did get out of the way.'

Räikkönen, as usual, did not appear to be overexcited by the incident, although he still made his point. 'I don't know how much time I lost,' he said. 'For sure, he could have found a slightly easier way to let me past, but what's happened has happened.'

Having heard this response from the Finn, Hamilton announced that he now felt ready to

become the first-ever rookie world champion. 'I'm here to do a completely clean job, rather than being investigated for one thing or another,' he insisted. 'I have to beat Fernando and Kimi. We have the pace. I'm confident and relaxed. It was close to a perfect last lap and a good battle with Felipe.'

In the end, he fell just 0.15 seconds behind Brazilian Massa, racing at his home track, while Räikkönen and Alonso trailed in third and fourth respectively. Afterwards, Hamilton was relaxed enough to make a joke about Friday's wet-tyre

scandal. 'It wasn't down to me,' he reminded people. 'I do what I'm told. We got a fine. Fortunately, I don't have to pay for it.'

Alonso was not so happy. 'I'm not being pessimistic, but my chances of winning the championship are less now after qualifying fourth,' he admitted. 'I need a special race if I want to be champion again.'

BELOW: Hard luck – fellow British driver David Coulthard consoles Lewis Hamilton after the rookie finishes in seventh place at the Brazilian Grand Prix and therefore second in the world drivers' championship.

All three would go to bed that night wondering what the next day would bring. Emerson Fittipaldi, a respected figure at Interlagos, reckoned the pressure was on the rookie's shoulders. 'If I was Alonso, I'd be thinking how nervous Hamilton will be when he could have won in China and didn't,' said the Brazilian former Formula One world champion.

But just before he retired to his hotel, Hamilton offered a different take on the situation. 'Being in the lead is where you want to be,' he said. 'If you're behind and you're losing points to someone who's pulling away from you, there's more pressure. You're happiest when you're leading and trying to defend the lead. I've had the experience of leading before. The difference is that this is the world championship. This is the fight to be the best driver in the world. It's always been my dream to be seen to be the best driver in the world.'

Overnight, the England rugby team lost out to South Africa in the Rugby World Cup final in Paris. It was the start of a weekend that had promised so much for British sport but in the end delivered two crushing blows. Hamilton's dreams were shattered on the Sunday afternoon at Interlagos – at least for the season. All he had to do was win enough points and keep close enough to his nearest rivals to take the championship, but his racing instincts got the better of him to the very end. The green lights shone to begin the Brazilian Grand Prix, and Massa on pole eased ahead. Directly behind him, Räikkönen, on the cleaner side of the track, shot inside Hamilton and into second place, blocking the rookie in the process. This allowed Alonso to zip past Hamilton on the inside so that when the cars reached turn three Hamilton had dropped from second to fourth. This should not have been a problem. If the positions had stayed as they were, Hamilton would have been world champion. But Lewis was not happy about being taken out by both the Finn and the Spaniard, and at the very next corner he attempted to overtake Alonso, locked his wheels and slid off the track. By the time he returned, he found himself down in eighth place.

This was a problem but not a crisis. The Ferraris were pulling away, but as long as Hamilton could reclaim three places he would still be crowned the first-ever rookie world champion. Most of the job was done after he took out first Jarno Trulli and then Nick Heidfeld. However, his grasp on the title was all

but lost on lap eight. Hamilton's McLaren suddenly, and without prior notice, lost all pace as the gearbox slammed into neutral and refused to move until he had slipped right down to 18th position. The middle-placed cars, and even some back markers, shot past as the McLaren, normally one of the fastest cars on the grid, resembled a milk float. Then, just as suddenly, the gearbox revved back into life, and the car was away again, albeit close to the back of the race. If Hamilton was to stand any chance of winning the title, it would require one of the great

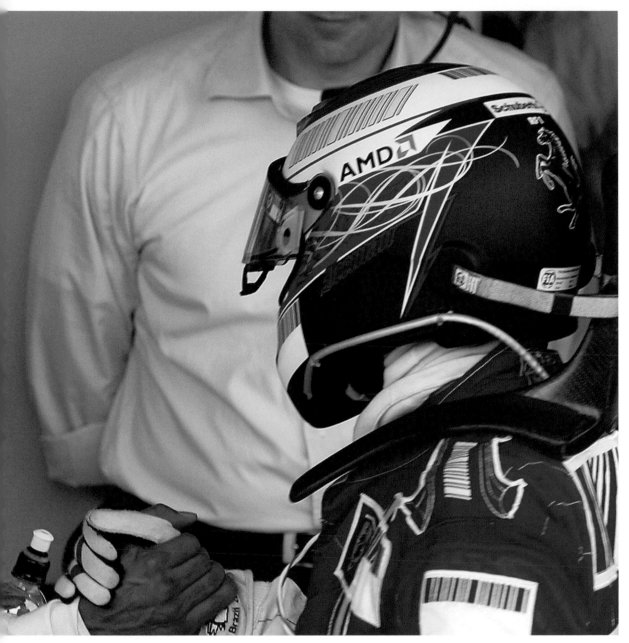

comebacks and ill luck befalling others. By lap 20, Hamilton had torn through half the field and was up to eleventh, and then tenth by his first pit stop. By lap 37 and a second stop at the pits after a short, low-fuel stint on soft tyres, he was lying in ninth place.

Meanwhile, the two Ferraris already had the race sewn up, but with Alonso labouring in third it was crucial that Räikkönen, as the only Ferrari driver able to win the world title, came first in Brazil. It was without question that race leader Massa, who had promised to help his teammate to become world

ABOVE: Hands of respect – new world champion Kimi Räikkönen and Lewis Hamilton, the man he beat by a single point, shake hands at the end of the Brazilian Grand Prix.

champion, would concede the race, even in his home city, but the team made it less obvious by ensuring the Finn emerged ahead of the Brazilian when both came into the pits.

With twelve laps remaining, Hamilton, who had just produced a fastest lap, reached eighth place, but he still needed to grab three positions. Ahead of him, the likes of Nico Rosberg in his Williams and Robert

Kubica and Nick Heidfeld in their BMW Saubers were flying. Hamilton managed to pass Jarno Trulli to take seventh place, but that was as good as it got. He trailed home in seventh, his third-worst result of the season. With Räikkönen winning the race and Alonso only managing third, the world title went to the Finn, with Hamilton one point behind, although he edged out Alonso, who was also on one hundred and nine points, by virtue of winning the same amount of Grands Prix (four) but claiming more second places during the season.

'I never gave up until I saw the chequered flag,' Hamilton said immediately afterwards, with a beaming smile disguising the pain. 'They told me on the radio that I could do it, and I believed it.'

Maybe, but in the end the ironic situation of the most reliable car on the circuit letting him down cost Lewis Hamilton a first-ever world title for a rookie. If that was a downside to the season, then the climax served up in Brazil was in keeping with the helter-skelter roller-coaster ride Formula One had provided in 2007. Kimi Räikkönen, with the fifteenth Grand Prix win of his career and sixth of the season, had been overdue a world championship, and few could begrudge him now, while Fernando Alonso followed up back-to-back world titles with a third place.

It had been quite a season, but thoughts had already turned to 2008 almost before the last engine had been shut down. With Lewis Hamilton gunning for that world title, and with Räikkönen and Alonso, wherever the Spaniard would end up, standing in his way, plus a wealth of young talent coming up fast on the ropes, including Robert Kubica, Nico Rosberg and Heikki Kovalainen, the future looked bright for Formula One. But most of all, the future looked bright for Lewis Hamilton. After all, the present was already magnificent.

RACE RESULT

	DRIVER	TEAM	POINTS
1	Kimi Räikkönen	Ferrari	10
2	Felipe Massa	Ferrari	8
3	Fernando Alonso	McLaren-Mercedes	6
4	Nico Rosberg	Williams	5
5	Robert Kubica	BMW Sauber	4
6	Nick Heidfeld	BMW Sauber	3
7	Lewis Hamilton	McLaren-Mercedes	2
8	Jarno Trulli	Toyota	1

CONSTRUCTORS' CHAMPIONSHIP AFTER SEVENTEEN RACES

	TEAM	POINTS
1	Ferrari	204
2	BMW Sauber	101
3	Renault	51
4	Williams	33
5	Red Bull	24
6	Toyota	13
7	Toro Rosso	8
8	Honda	6
9	Super Aguri	4
10	Spyker	1

DRIVERS' CHAMPIONSHIP AFTER SEVENTEEN RACES

	DRIVER	POINTS
1	Kimi Räikkönen	110
2	Lewis Hamilton	109
3	Fernando Alonso	109
4	Felipe Massa	94
5	Nick Heidfeld	61
6	Robert Kubica	39
7	Heikki Kovalainen	30
8	Giancarlo Fisichella	21
9	Nico Rosberg	20
10	David Coulthard	14
11	Alex Wurz	13
12	Mark Webber	10
13	Jarno Trulli	8
14	Sebastian Vettel	6
15	Jenson Button	6
16	Ralf Schumacher	5
17	Takuma Sato	4
18	Vitantonio Liuzzi	3
19	Adrian Sutil	1

FACING PAGE: The great inquisition – the world's media asks how could it go so wrong as Lewis Hamilton fulfils his post-race duties at Interlagos.

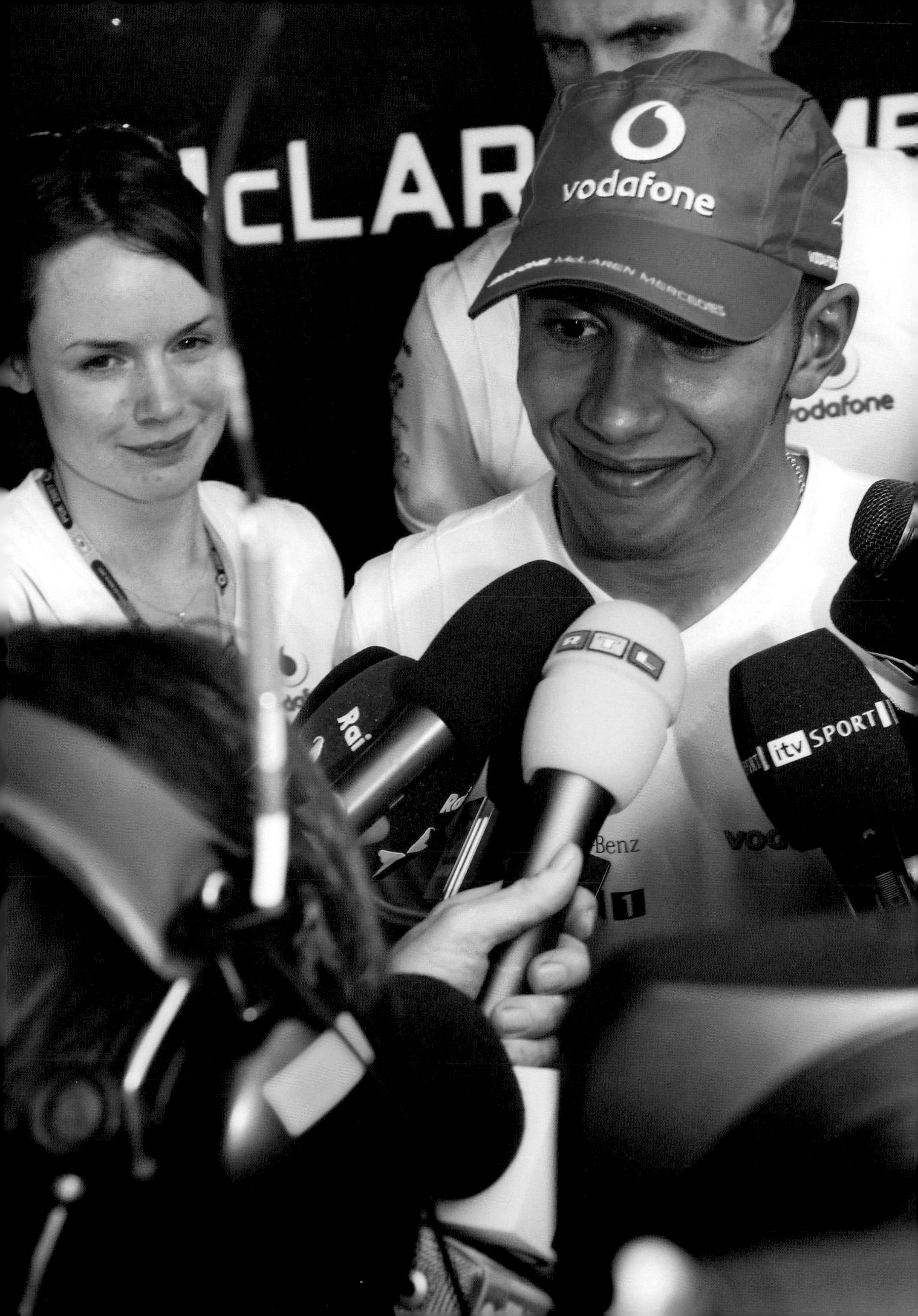
vodafone
vodafone
RTL
Rai
itv SPORT

Conclusion

The drama was still not over. An inquiry into the temperature of the petrol in the cars that finished fourth, fifth and sixth suddenly gave Hamilton a glimmer of hope. A decision to exclude the Williams of Nico Rosberg and the BMW Saubers of Robert Kubica and Nick Heidfeld from the Brazilian Grand Prix would have promoted Hamilton from seventh to fourth, which would have handed him five points, instead of two, and a two-point advantage over Räikkönen at the end of the season. The petrol in the three cars was found to have been cooled to a temperature below the level permissible under Formula One's regulations (10 °C below the ambient temperature), but after five hours of deliberation it was decided that no action would be taken. It was another opportunity, however unsatisfactory, that went begging.

Lewis Hamilton learned more in one season than many drivers do in their whole careers. Two races before the Brazilian Grand Prix, the British driver had led the world championship by twelve points, and it seemed as though the title was surely coming back to the UK for the first time in eleven years. Then a disastrous weekend in China – virtually from start to finish – brought the championship down to the wire at Interlagos. Despite this, the cards were still heavily stacked in Hamilton's favour.

It was not to be. Having led the drivers' title race outright from the Canadian Grand Prix back in May, he was pipped at the post by Kimi Räikkönen 11 races later. Yet the manner in which Hamilton handled what must have been a huge blow was remarkable. 'Obviously, I'm pretty disappointed, having led for so much of the season,' he admitted as he sat in the McLaren-Mercedes motorhome surrounded by downcast team members. 'But you have to put it into perspective. This is my first year in Formula One, and overall it has been phenomenal. Next year, I'll bounce back. I went into the race saying that whatever happens today, it's been an amazing year. Who would have thought I would have been leading the world championship at this stage? It's been a huge roller-coaster ride. For sure, we all wanted to win. We wanted to win the Rugby World Cup. I wanted to win the world championship. It's clearly not England's turn this year.'

It was a good effort by the 22 year old to hide his emotions, but a man who was born to win, and was used to winning, knew a golden chance to make history had just evaporated in front of him. 'Somebody doesn't want me to win this,' he suggested, with a weak smile. 'I made one mistake. It wasn't a great start. I locked up behind Fernando to avoid hitting him then went wide. I was still quite relaxed, knowing that I had the pace to regain position. Apart from my first lap, I think I drove one of my best races.'

What happened next had nothing to do with Hamilton and a great deal to do with ill luck. He was to all intents and purposes a faulty gear shift away from winning the world championship. 'I was downshifting into turn four, and the car just slammed into neutral,' he explained. 'I coasted for a long time, and then, eventually, I don't know how, it clicked back in. From then on, we had to manage the engine. But I didn't feel it was over until the chequered flag.'

Well, that was almost true. He did admit to one moment of doubt when his car had become the slowest vehicle on the circuit. 'When I was coasting, I thought someone didn't want me to win the championship,' he revealed. 'I've had tyre problems, there was my mistake in the last race and then something happened again in this race. But that is racing, I guess. I go into next year full of confidence. I really can't wait. I'll be a lot stronger and even better prepared. I have the experience now. I can bank that and start from fresh in Melbourne. I was a bit emotional when I crossed the line, but I can't deny it's been a fantastic season. I finished second in the world championship and beat my teammate under extremely difficult circumstances. That was a goal and a great result. Kimi drove well and deserves the title.'

Anthony, his equally inspirational father, was just as upbeat, perhaps even more so. He may have been desperately disappointed at the season's outcome, but he preferred to look at the positives and to dream about a future that promises so much. 'None of us are in pain,' he insisted. 'We feel great. You've just seen the most fantastic season in Formula One ever. At the start of the year, we would have taken third or fourth. It's a happy day. Don't mourn. It's been an awesome season. Lewis has handled so much this season with a smile on his face. I'm really proud of my son for what he has done.

'We'll be coming back stronger next season after this. I'm sure we'll be giving the champion a run for his money. We have many years in this business. There's no rush. We didn't win it this year, and if we don't win it next year, then we'll win the world title the year after that. One thing's for sure: Lewis Hamilton is here to stay. We're going to be a force to reckon with for a long time and hopefully without all the rubbish we've had to endure this season.'

Ron Dennis was ashen-faced at the end of it all. He had seen some interesting and controversial seasons in his time as boss of McLaren but none of them

BELOW: The weekend of the Brazilian Grand Prix didn't turn out as hoped for English sport.

could have compared to 2007. Thrown out of the constructors' championship after the Spygate scandal had labelled his team as cheats, and in and out of FIA hearings, appeals and stewards' meetings as the season lurched towards its dramatic climax, he would have at least expected to have landed the drivers' world title, especially with one of his men leading the other by four points and Kimi Räikkönen three points further back. Instead, and for only the second time since the Formula One world championship began 57 years earlier, the man who began the last Grand Prix of the season in third place went on to win the day and win the world championship.

Most of all, Dennis felt abject disappointment for the young man he had nurtured from an early age. 'We've got to have a sporting attitude to the outcome,' Dennis said. 'I'm struggling to find words right now. Lewis enjoyed phenomenal reliability from his car all season until now. The gearbox selected neutral and wouldn't budge for a while, but after that our three-stop strategy picked up ten seconds to the point that we only needed two cars to stop. It's not about one race. It's about the whole championship. We as a team feel very proud of our achievements this season and the way in which we have conducted ourselves. To come into this showdown with two drivers in with a chance of winning the world championship is testament to the hard work and dedication everybody in the team has put in throughout this difficult year. Now we have to congratulate Kimi and look forward.'

Räikkönen, who had been seventeen points behind Hamilton with two races remaining, is not exactly known for showing his emotions, but even the 'Iceman' was taken aback by his turnaround in fortune. 'We were not in a strong position, but we always believed we could recover,' said the man who had taken over from Michael Schumacher at Ferrari and walked away with a world title. 'Even in the hard times, we stuck together. We didn't give up. We kept cool heads, and we've ended up winning both the constructors' and drivers' world titles. It's been perfect teamwork, especially from Felipe, who's been a big help to me.

'The start was so important. The main thing was to get past Hamilton, which I managed to do right at the start. Then when I saw in my mirror that Hamilton had gone off, I knew we were in with a chance. Even when I crossed the finish line and took the chequered flag, it took a long time to hear we'd finally won the world championship. It's been an amazing day and an amazing season.'

It certainly had, and former British legends of the track were quick to throw their support behind Lewis Hamilton. 'Lewis will be disappointed, but he will regroup quickly,' said Damon Hill. 'He has shown more potential as a newcomer this year than any rookie driver has ever done. We should celebrate this great performance and achievement. The worrying thing for the other drivers is that he's only going to get better.'

Murray Walker, the former voice of Formula One, also praised the rookie. 'I'm sorry for Lewis,' said Walker. 'For someone who is usually so focused, I think the pressure got to him. But it's not a question of if Lewis can win a world championship, it's when.'

Sir Stirling Moss – like Hamilton, a true racer in his time – was another motor-racing legend who found positive words for the young driver. 'The record books will tell us Kimi Räikkönen was the 2007 world champion, but Lewis deserved it,' he insisted. 'He is an extremely impressive young man. He is Fangio and Senna rolled into one. How good can he be? He only has to iron out those minor mistakes, and his time will come – and soon. Of that I am absolutely sure.'

There was probably nobody in Formula One who disagreed with that statement. It had been an extraordinary season and an extraordinary story; perhaps, though, it would have been just a little too far-fetched to have ended with a first-ever rookie world champion. Nobody is likely to forget the 2007 Formula One season in a hurry, and if the 2008 season proves to be half as good as its predecessor, the world of sport is destined for another incredible year.

As for Lewis Hamilton, the boy who grew up on a council estate in Stevenage in a broken home, who became the first black man ever to race a Formula One car, who was the first-ever driver to record nine back-to-back podium places in his first nine races and whose father held down three jobs to try to make ends meet has proved that if you have the will and the belief, absolutely anything in life is possible. And if that sounds like the end of the story, nothing could be further from the truth. The story of Lewis Hamilton, despite everything that has already happened in his amazing life, has only just begun.

| OVERLEAF: The future looks bright for Lewis Hamilton.

alg